THE WAR OF 1920

Shaemas O'Sheel

Illustrated by:

A. Staehle

Preface by:

Chris Langer

Chris Langer 2017

Printed in the United States of America

Library of Congress Control Number: 2017908542

ISBN: 1545146187
ISBN-13: 978-1545146187

To my loving parents,

Janice and Eric

CONTENTS

Preface

I came across "The War of 1920" while doing research for a paper regarding German-American thought for a graduate class. While scouring the German-American Newspaper *The Fatherland*, I began noticing little bits that referenced an international war in 1920. Given that the particular paper was published in 1915, I was intrigued. As I steadily pieced the various articles together, I came to realize that this was in fact a book.

"The War of 1920" is an alternate-history by Irish-American nationalist Shaemas O'Sheel, detailing a timeline where the Allies of the Great War have invaded the unsuspecting United States of America. With enemies invading from all sides, many Americans are dumbfounded at how such a cataclysmic event could happen. The story is told via the diary of Gustav Bauerfeldt, a war correspondent of the fictional German newspaper *Berliner Rundschau*. Bauerfeldt describes the events that have befallen the United States, from the various battles to the personalities involved. The book can be seen as a reaction to the growing breaches of neutrality America seemed to make in 1915.

When the book was originally published in 1915, the conflict between the Entente and the Central Powers was still under a year old. However, the horrors of mechanized warfare were beginning to set in for the American people. Europe was tearing itself asunder; its lands riddled with craters and littered with the corpses of the once proud youth. Americans could but watch in abject horror as the old world effectively collapsed before them. A healthy amount of Americans were supporters of the Entente, or the Allies, at this time. This was largely the result of a shared Anglo-Saxon heritage from Colonial times. This support would solidify when, shortly after hostilities erupted, England cut the communications cable from Berlin to New York. Any news of the war coming into the United States would have to go through Entente censors.

What followed was a slew of anti-German propaganda, depicting the Germans as barbarians committing atrocities across neutral Belgian's landscape, including an unsubstantiated claim that German soldiers had opened fire on members of the Red Cross. Germany was unable to defend itself against the rising

propaganda onslaught. Several German-American writers, such as
Frederick F. Schrader, protested the Germanophobic nature of the
press. Schrader himself noted the irony of the lines many
American newspapers were taking in his article "The
Germanophobe Press," calling it hyperbolic that that the
supposedly freedom-loving American media was exalting the
despotic "semi-barbarous Russia" over the German state.[1]

"The War of 1920," while ultimately propaganda, is notable
for the voicing the fears many Americans were feeling in 1915.
The country was seething as a result of the *Lusitania* disaster and
seemed to be inching closer to war with the Central Powers as a
result. United States intervention in the Mexican Civil War was
expanding, and many Americans feared the rumored growing
influence of the Japanese within the region. In addition, American
munitions trade to the Allies grew by the day, with anti-
interventionists lamenting the increasingly pro-Allies neutrality the
United States was drifting towards. The book references these
events often, except with the United States being on the receiving

[1]Schrader, Frederick K. "The Germanophobe Press." *The Fatherland* (New York), August 10, 1914, Volume 1., No. 1. 6.

end of them. This was designed to serve as a way to look at the present war with a different lens, and it forces readers to look at how it would seemingly feel to be in the shoes of the Germans.

While the United States would ultimately enter World War I in 1917 after years of prolonged tensions with Germany, "The War of 1920" serves as a fascinating piece of historical writing that conveyed the thoughts and fears many anti-interventionist Americans felt at the time. I hope that present readers will appreciate this rather unique look into the mind of one such author.

-Chris Langer, May 2017

Shaemas O'Sheel

The English Navy Cuts the Cable

I

(Being the Diary of Gustav Bauerfeldt, War Correspondent of the Berliner Rundschau)

he United States at war! The United States at war with the Allies! The United States at war with England, Japan, Russia, and France! These phrases had rung in my mind for weeks, fascinating me like some scrap of futuristic free verse, terrible in their irony. The United States at war, battling like a giant suddenly attacked and overthrown by merciless enemies, who but a moment before smiled through a mask of friendship, but now struck to the heart, from every side!

From the moment the news flashed across the cables, I had sought my paper's permission to go to America, but sought in vain. The general attitude throughout Germany was one of indifference mingled with satisfaction. "The Allies have fallen out among themselves–!" said the Germans, with a shrug of the shoulders, a natural feeling enough feeling when we think how many of them still mourned for sons, husbands, fathers and lovers stricken down by American bullets and American shrapnel. But I had many kindly memories of America, despite the hard things I had had to endure during the mad days of the Summer of 1915. I wanted to learn the truth and tell it to the German people. I realized that they were being made the dupes of English control of the news, like the American people during the Great War.

The first act of the English navy had been to cut the American cables, while British spies wrecked the two wireless plants, at Tuckerton and Sayville, which alone communicated with another country other than England, and thenceforth all news of events in the Western Hemisphere had come from Fleet Street. What was fact, what was falsification, what was fiction, we could only guess.

London, July 19th: Reports from many points along the border of the States reveal such chaos and panic that it is doubted whether any prolonged resistance will be offered to the Allied forces. The inhabitants of all the large Eastern cities are fleeing by the hundred thousand and taking refuge in the wilderness bordering the Ohio and Mississippi Rivers. Numerous fatal accidents attended the flight from New York. The Brooklyn Bridge yesterday gave way beneath the weight of refugees with appalling loss of life. A score of trains became jammed in the Pennsylvania Railroad Tunnel and one of them caught fire from the inevitable Yankee smoke. Thousands of men, women, and children were trapped and suffocated. A number of ferry boats have sunk. All of the wealthier inhabitants who did not fly the first day have been attacked by poor denizens of the East Side, who took their motors from them and sacked their houses.

Caracas, Venezuela, July 21st: The Southern States of the American Union are now feeling the weight of retribution for their centuries of oppression of the negroes. The blacks have everywhere risen and defeated the whites with great losses. White men, women, and children are being herded in concentration camps, and a negro Republic has been erected, with its Capital at Birmingham. A negro army is advancing to join the Japanese-Mexican Allies who have already invaded Texas.

Halifax, July 24th: The Canadian, Hindu, and Japanese troops have continued to win successes East and West. The capture of New York City is imminent.

Tokyo, July 24th: The Japanese forces are now in complete control of the States of Washington, Oregon, and Texas. Regiments of Japanese reservists from South America are landing in California. The Japanese fleet has completely blockaded the Pacific Coast. Three more American ships were captured yesterday in the Southern Pacific.

London, July 25th: In answer to a question by Mr. Herbert Wilkes in the House yesterday, as to proposals for the partition and government of North America, Mr. Asquith said: "I am not at liberty now, as the honorable gentlemen will understand, to discuss the matter fully. I am happy to state that our interests and those of our Allies do not at any point conflict. The natural aspirations of Russia for the seaboard of Alaska must be carefully considered, as well as the insistence of Canada on the rectification of the

Canadian-Alaskan frontier. The main interests of our Japanese allies are on the Pacific Coast. It will doubtless be found convenient to place the greater part of the States under the direct administration of the Colonial Office, but the union of certain border states with Canada naturally suggests itself. We are aware of the prevalence in many States of a very friendly feeling towards us and we expect that the inhabitants of these States, being of our own blood and tradition, sharing with us Anglo-Saxon ideals and the English Bible, will be only too glad to dissociate themselves from those States where alien stocks have hindered the advance of civilization., as soon as our troops are in full possession. If we can break up the Union into its constituent States we can do as we like."

Replying to a question as to what measures the military authorities would take to suppress sniping, which has occurred in many places, Lord Kitchener replied: "Military necessity knows no law except its own, which must be stern and thorough. We shall take any repressive steps which the situation may make necessary."

London, August 7th: The Admiralty has announced that the *Queen Elizabeth* and the *Overpowering* have bombarded and silenced the Sandy Hook fortifications. A ship laden with

Argentine beef, attempting to run the blockade, was captured.

"London, August 7th, 1920–The War Office has announced that sniping occurred at Rochester, whereupon Gen. Hughes ordered the city destroyed"

The War Office has announced that sniping occurred at

Rochester, whereupon General Hughes, commanding the Canadian

army, ordered the city destroyed. Our Japanese Allies have taken similar measures at North Yakima, Washington.

Making what discount I could, these reports were disquieting enough. There could be no doubt about the fate of Rochester, North Yakima, and other places mentioned in other dispatches. The vengeance taken was thorough and relentless. I thought of Louvain, where he had destroyed but a sixth of the town, carefully discriminating between those streets whence sniping had come, and those of which had remained quiet. I marveled at Premier Asquith's use, word for word, of a phrase Kitchener had used about the German Empire in 1914: "If we can break up the Union into its constituents States, we can do as we like."

Everyone in Germany had thought that the end had come when the news of the capture of the whole American Eastern Army was reported. But when, a few days later, grudging English reports, pieced together with scant items from South America, told of the dispersion of the first two divisions of the Canadian invaders by a volunteer army under Congressman Shawn O'Hagan, my paper, aware of my previous acquaintance with this young statesman who had suddenly turned General, bade me catch the Hamburg-

American liner *President Lincoln* and proceed to the front.

The Imperial Government had promised England that our liners would carry nothing that was contraband according to accepted International Law, but would carry anything else they pleased, and England's navy dared not even challenge us as we passed them, some hundred miles from the American coast, but all other ships they held up wherever they found them.

We sailed past Sandy Hook, into that harbor which for a century had known no rest. Now the waters were quiet and the myriad of masts that rose above the piers actually seemed cobwebbed. The streets of New York were full of excited crowds, and soldiers in a variety of uniforms drilled in the parks. I had little time then, however, to see or hear much. A young Captain had been ordered by General O'Hagan to meet me. He showed me the itinerary he had been given. "The Erie to Calicoon: to Jeffersonville, Liberty, Neversink, and Grahamsville. Unless you hurry you will be caught."

We hurried. A special train of one car did its best in an excited sort of way over a poor road. At one place we passed a few ammunition and provision trains. At dusk we alighted at Calicoon.

A racing car with uniformed chauffeur awaited us. For hours we tore through a night of dim star-light, over roads that threatened to disintegrate the car. Suddenly shots were heard; then long volleys. Out of the terrifying rattle sounded the hoofs of a cavalry company which tore past us. A Captain saw us and gave the order to halt. My escort greeted him as a dozen rifles covered us. Down went the guns, and after a moment's talk, on we went with the troop around us. At the top of the ridge I suddenly discerned a line of trenches, manned by infantry. There the cavalry stopped, but we raced on till we came to a village where dim companies moved about, lit only by fitful flashes from electric pocket-lights.

Sore and shaken, I was helped out of the car and lifted to a horse. For another hour we climbed, climbed, toward a dimly-marked hilltop. Firing went on everywhere to the South. A great hulk of a hill rose to the West of us, three or four miles away. There seemed to be two long lines of trenches running from top to bottom. They spat fire at each other incessantly. Farther to the South, the rattle of riflery was continuous. Shells hurled toward our hill, exploding with dull flashes. They fell short, stopped; there was no reply from the American lines. I wondered if this volunteer army had guns. I wondered how much ammunition they had for their rifles. And while I wondered, I came face to face with General O'Hagan.

The March of Events

II

We were on the hill-top. The General swept the horizon with a gesture. "On a clear day," he said, "you can see from here to Pennsylvania and to Massachusetts. You look over typical American country. There are farms, rather ill-cultivated, and little towns, spasmodically progressive. There are people whose ancestors, Dutch, German, Irish and English, cleared the Indians from these valleys, and there are new settlements of Jewish farmers. In summer the myriads of the city fled here for fresh air. And now a little army of Americans fights against a host of Canadians, bitter with the hatred bred in them by their Anglo-maniac press, and aided by corps of Hindus and Japanese! And two thousand miles away greater hosts, chiefly brown men and yellow men, ravage the fertile valleys of the Pacific Coast and the 'Inland Empire.' To the South, swarms of Mexicans and Japs are sweeping through Texas to Louisiana. New Orleans trembles under the guns of English and French cruisers. They will sail up the Mississippi; they will cut off the grain and cotton States. The thousand-mile border from Lakes to the Rockies is harried daily by their cavalry, and we do not know where they will strike with the Sikhs and Ghurkas.

"Thanks to our acts while you were in your life-and-death struggle a few years ago, Britannia still rules the waves. The Great Sea-Serpent, and the Little Sea-Serpent of the Pacific, holds us tightly in their coils. At any moment the English fleet may overwhelm the defences of New York. Tonight American women and girls are subject to the lust of Asiatics, while tens of thousands of American homes lie in ruins, and their protectors lie in their blood. In the end we my exterminate these armies from the vast bosom of America; but while those invincible navies watch our shores, we can win peace only at the cost of all our outlying possessions, our own border territory, our influence in this Hemisphere, and a ransom that will beggar us."

"Swarms of Mexicans and Japs are sweeping through Texas to Louisiana."

He passed and turned to me. "There can be help from but one quarter. Germany alone can save us. Do you think we can hope—?"

"I am afraid not," I answered. Suddenly, a rocket shot up from the hill opposite, then another; then a third.

"They are placing their heavy artillery on the other side of Thunder Hill," said General O'Hagan. "Go to bed. Tomorrow or the next day we will leave here. The fighting is over for tonight.

I lay on a couch of hemlock boughs covered by blankets, but for long I did not sleep. I thought of this war and of the last war in which my country had faced the powers which now assaulted America. I remembered how completely we had beaten them in military operations, only to find the war dragging out cruelly because of England's autocracy of the sea. As if it had been a lake within her shores, Britannia ruled the Atlantic with regard to nothing but her own will–and, eventually, our submarines. The American Government had feebly debated with Sir Edward Grey the academic rights and wrongs of England's acts, all the while letting it be known that America would acquiesce in all that

England chose to do.

The United States suffered incredibly by the operation of the English blockade, conducted close to the ports of America and far from Germany; thousands were ruined in the South while English cotton speculators fattened; mills were closed in the North for want of German dye-stuffs; mines and factories shut down with the shutting down of the German market for peaceful industrial raw minerals and products. But the press, controlled by Wall Street, mortgaged by English money-lenders, or owned by men interested in Steel and in ammunition and powder works, concealed the wide distress. Then the great bargain was made between the American money lords and the English. J.P. Morgan was made the agent of the British Government, at a huge commission, to supply it with munitions; whereupon the Stock Exchange re-opened on a boom created by war orders, the English speculators, caught in August, 1914, overloaded with securities, were enabled to unload, and the munitions-ring was able to buy at beautifully low figures.

The public conscience of America was aroused against this blood-stained traffic; monster meetings were held everywhere, religious bodies protested, and petitions deluged Congressmen.

Germany also was aroused, and reminded the American Government that while it had every right to permit this arming of the Allies, it was under no compulsion to do so; that to do so was, in the circumstances, effectively unneutral; and that if the export of such means of war from America ceased, thousands of lives and incalculable human agony may be spared.

The reply of the American Administration will be remembered. Germany was thereupon compelled to protect herself against American bullets, shells, guns and armored cars by adopting methods which, long within her power, she had hitherto refrained from. The *Lusitania,* the pride of the Cunard Line, sailing under the orders of the English Admiralty, laden with ammunition and carrying English reservists and English munitions-contractors, was torpedoed; the ammunition in her hold exploded and she sank from that explosion in ten minutes, though she could have floated an hour had she suffered merely the blow of a torpedo. About a thousand English subjects and one hundred Americans perished. The German Government at once issued statements to the world in general and to the United States in particular, setting forth all the facts; the American authorities nevertheless protested in threatening notes which calmly ignored the belligerent character of the vessel and her cargo, and assumed that she was a peaceful passenger ship! The notes were in fact a demand that Germany cease to use submarines.

My readers will remember our calm but inflexible replies, and also the unfortunate period of tension between the United States and Germany which followed. After that came the amazing events of the Autumn, culminating in the hasty Peace of Brussels, by which Germany retained Antwerp, as well as the Baltic Provinces of Russia; Russian Poland was united to Galacia as an autonomous State under the guardianship of Germany and Austria-Hungary; Turkey retained Constantinople, and England retained control of Egypt after recognizing anew the suzerainty of Turkey, while Germany was given a free hand in Mesopotamia.

But, in spite of the holding of Antwerp and the treaty provisions guaranteeing her right to building a navy without answering anyone for it, Germany had to face the fact that England still retained control of the seas. France, drained of blood, was inarticulate; Russia was inflamed against England; and England herself at once began, with all the resources of her unrivalled art of

Publicity, to try and cultivate the friendship of Germany. It was, like most treaties of peace, thoroughly unsatisfactory to everybody, but under it Europe had lived now for four and a half years. Meanwhile, events in American had taken strange courses.

In the next chapter I shall present selections from the English and Japanese White papers of 1920, and from other private public documents, displaying the diplomatic preliminaries of the war.

How the Ring of Iron Was Forged

III

EXTRACT from the *Congressional Record,* November 18, 1916. In the House, H. 322, a Bill to Create a National Defense Board, under discussion.

MR. O'HAGAN: "Mr. Speaker, I am in accord with the views of the last two speakers as to the present armament policy of the United States, which one of them has summed up as imbecile and the other as criminal. Our army is now recruited to barely its legal strength, and there are fewer than 40,000 mobile troops in the United States, less than 700 field guns, not a single mobile big gun, barely enough ammunition for two days of battle, a serious shortage of coastal defense reserves, a militia crudely disciplined and ill-equipped as ever. As to the Navy, we grudgingly build one first-class battle cruiser, two dreadnaughts, and three first-class submarines a year.

"Mr. Speaker, as the House has nothing to say about foreign affairs, in the usual course, I ask your indulgence for a few remarks about the inter-relations of national preparedness and foreign problems.

"A year ago it was the fashion to believe that our only possible enemy was Germany. We have now, happily, concluded a treaty with that national adjusting all differences and laying a foundation for future friendship. The atmosphere is heavy with the incense burnt to the idea of Perpetual Peace. Every newspaper in the land is becoming one or another of the Peace movements. Mr. Carnegie has added $5,000,000 more to his endowment for Peace. Mr. John Hays Hammond exhibits his model of an International Court throughout the country. Proposals are before Congress for this nation to lead the way toward disarmament. These ideas are warmly praised in the *Bulletin of the Japan Society* and in the English press. Dr. David Starr Jordan is just as certain now that the last war has been fought as he was before August, 1914. We are in a very debauch of peaceful anticipations, and yet, Mr. Speaker–I see the terrible shadows of war creeping upon us!

"Mr. Speaker, on September 11, 1897, the *Saturday Review* of London published an article by Sir Alfred Mond, pointing out how inevitable war with Germany was, because, he said, 'Nations have fought for years over a city or a right of succession; must they not fight for two hundred and fifty million pounds of yearly commerce?' Much as I abhor the selfishness of that attitude, I cherish that article as a proof, in the light of what came to pass, that *wars are fought for causes.* If there are no causes for war between this country and others, we will have no war. *If there are causes, we must fight!*

"And there are causes! Consider Mexico; a territory vaster than any European country save Russia, abounding in wealth, inhabited by 16,000,000 Indians rapidly returning to a state of barbarism lower than in which Cortez found them! The exploiting

31

countries of the world look upon Mexico as a field for exploitation; and England and Japan are the only exploiting countries that can think of Mexico now, for Germany is fully occupied in Mesopotamia. England still controls every strategic point, save Antwerp, upon the seven seas; but her control of the Panama Canal from her West Indian Islands does not satisfy her. Already she has sounded us on the proposition to neutralize the Canal.

Japan calmly continues her exploitation of Mexico. From each successive revolutionary president she purchases more concessions. She has cajoled us into silence about her base in Turtle Bay. On the other hand, it is a matter of but a few years till the economic conditions created for us by our lack of merchant marine and our now complete exclusion from Mexico will inevitably conflict with Mexico in the Caribbean and Japan in the Pacific.

"Sir, our policy should include the creation of a merchant marine at any cost, the restoration of Tolls Exemption at Panama, the building of a Navy adequate to awe Japan and cause England to pause, and the firm insistence of our acquisition, by purchase or other means, of the British West Indies, British Honduras, and

British Guinea, and all of Canada that lies between our artificial northeastern border and our natural border, the St. Lawrence. To do these things might mean war; not to do them certainly means a war of humiliation for us.

"We shall someday have two navies blockading our coasts, while Englishmen, Canadians, Asiatics, and Mexicans will flow across our borders, in accordance with the plans which have been openly discussed by English, Canadian and Australian papers, and privately gloated over by the people of those lands ever since Sir Wilfrid Laurier, on January 28, 1908, reminded Canadians, in a speech in the House of Commons, that the day would come when they would welcome the Japanese fleet and the Japanese forces sailing into Vancouver to join them in war against their enemies."

The Bill to Create a National Defense Board was defeated, 329 to 37.

Extracts from an editorial in the Washington *Post*, Nov. 1, 1916:

"It's best for all Americans who appreciate the vast stake which this country has in China, to abandon hope that the present

Administration will make an eleventh hour attempt to protect our interests there. It was hoped that the conclusion of peace in Europe would free the timorous hands of the State Department, but that hope has died. It is hard to believe that anyone could have been other than willfully blind to the purposes of Japan. She aided England, in a way singularly little to England's advantage, and she aided Russia by facilitating the import into that country of America munitions of war, with the definite object of tying their hands while she bullied China into concessions which mean, in plain language, that Japan and Japan alone exploits and rules Southern Manchuria, Eastern Inner Mongolia, Shantung and other districts, that Japan has estopped China from granting concessions, territorial or commercial, at tide-water or inland, to any other nation, and that Japan has a finger in every political, financial, and military activity of the so-called Chinese Republic.

And now Japan appoints Count Terauchi Chief Resident of Pekin—Count Terauchi, whose mere presence in Korea was so terrible that the rules of Korea offered their country to Japan! In Pekin he will be all that Lord Cromer was in Egypt…What will England do?…Is the Pacific henceforth a Japanese lake?

From *Current Opinion,* December, 1916:

"To sum it up, President Wilson was re-elected because the impression of superior morality and elevated patriotism which his administration has made on great numbers of voters are sufficient to overcome dissatisfaction with economic conditions and the resentment against his foreign policy felt by large classes of people….In foreign affairs the next administration will display the same tendencies as the present: a marked friendship for England, and, despite the absence of Mr. Bryan, those pacific tendencies which were only interrupted during the tension with Germany, including discouragement of increased armaments."

From a Secret Document found in the Foreign Office in London during the German occupation in 1921. Duplicate of Dispatch from Sir Edward Grey to Sir E. Goschen, British Ambassador at Tokyo:

"June 15, 1918. I regret that your negotiations have been no more successful than those of Sir H. Rumbold at Berlin, but I confess that I have had to anticipate that Germany would not join us in representations directed against Japan, and that Japan would not retreat an inch. Obviously, there are but two courses open to us. One is to break with Japan and take steps to make her acknowledge our supremacy and yield to our wishes. The other is to agree, for the present, to divide the Pacific with her. I do not see how we can avoid choosing the latter course. Indeed, Japan is capable of planning so secretly and striking so suddenly that we, with our vital interests in India, China, and Australasia, are in no position safely to oppose her when she is not involved elsewhere.

Fortunately, Japan has every disposition to become involved in America, and this presents us two opportunities. In the first place, Japan's interests and ours as to the United States, the Panama Canal, and Mexico are identical. In the second place, if we go into those matters with Japan, we can contrive to keep our hands free enough to regain ascendancy in the Pacific while her whole power is peremptorily engaged in America. You say that the sentiments of the great masses of patriotic Japanese are with difficulty restrained; and my problem is greatly clarified by your assurances that the Japanese Government needs only our encouragement to adopt an aggressive policy as to Japanese exploitation in Mexico and Japanese rights in California. Eventuations at Mexico and Panama will force our intervention, and the time will be ripe for us to assert our dominant rights in the Caribbean.

EDWARD GREY PLANS THE PARTITION OF AMERICA

"If we can break up the Union into constituent parts, we can do as we like."

I have gone over all this with our chief political and financial advisers, and it is agreed that the time draws near when our present effective financial control of the United States must be used to assure English ascendancy on the Western Hemisphere and English hegemony of all waters and divisions in the Atlantic. This is part of our historic destiny, which the Revolution of 1776 interrupted but did not change. Of course, before we could enter such a wat, much must be done to assure protection to the British capital in the States and to perfect in Canada those preparations long since begun in Vancouver and Halifax. Much more must be done to prepare public opinion here.

It will also be necessary for us and Japan to continue to purchase as much as possible of the output of American munitions factories, and to continue to draw them under the control of English capital. Our present liberal purchasing has prevented the American munitions makers from lending any support to the few American agitators for increased armaments. The peace movement dominates the States, ably directed by the board nominated in the will of the late Mr. Carnegie. Very possibly the unpreparedness of the United States, due to these teachings and lack of munitions caused by our purchasing, may give us an easy victory without the necessity of following our words with blows. "This is for your guidance in the new conversations with Baron Kato.

I am, etc., E. GREY."

From Editorial in the Hearst paper, December 1, 1918:

"The people of the United States have been rudely awakened from their dream of peace and security. Like a bolt from the blue, the new Japanese demands have rent the heavens of our complacency....The people of California have a right to demand an end to this. It is not merely that their sovereign rights and dignities are repeatedly outraged. They know that the Japanese Government is not bullying them for the fun of it. They realize that behind these demands is a purpose as steadily pursued as Japan has pursued all those policies which has made her a powerful nation. The people of the whole country should heed the warning of California....

"There is evident here a balancing of issues. Japan expects us to yield in Mexico as the price of peace in California. And if we do not yield in Mexico, the Californian issue will be her excuse for taking what she wants by whatever means she chooses. We must yield or fight."

From the New York Evening *Post*, May 5, 1919:

"The excellent beginnings made by the American-Japanese Arbitration Commission are a source of gratification for all Americans. When the Japanese note was presented last Winter many doubtless were puzzled and frightened; but it is greatly to our credit that only the Hearst newspapers and a few local prints in California beat the jingo drum. The vast majority of our press recognized that it would be just as great a calamity for us to drift into strained relations with Japan as to revive our happily buried differences with England."

From *The International*, July, 1919:

"...The significant thing which the people of this country cannot know, and which the press, in a criminal conspiracy of silence, conceals from them, is the constantly growing volume and intensity of hostile comment in England. It is all singularly of a pattern–or rather, of three patterns. First, there are articles by self-styled authorities on America, deriding and denouncing this, that and the other thing in American life and history. Second, there are references, gradually becoming more emphatic, to the necessity of securing of England her full rights in the Caribbean and Mexico.

Third, there are editorials, and a bias in news-items, supporting the Japanese contentions....

"It was not supposed to be that English public opinion would unanimously support an alignment of the Empire with Japan against us. On the contrary, there was to be expected a great deal of indignant denunciation of such an alignment. So here we have the same secret, malignant influence which rigged the press of the world against Germany, in anticipation of a war in which Hindu, Jap, Turko, and Senegalese were hurled against that white nation, now rigging the press of the world against us. Is it in anticipation of a war in which Hindu, Jap, Turko, and Senegalese are to be hurled against us?"

English White Paper, No. 21. Sir E. Grey to Sir E. Goschen. March 2, 1920:

"I have had an interview with the American Ambassador, who came to inquire what the attitude of England would be if the negotiations between Japan and the United States should fail. I assured him that the attitude of His Majesty's Government was that of a sincere friend of both nations, with no interest in the points at issue and no desire but to be of service in the preservation of good relations. I reminded him of our natural affection for the United States, which, as he stated some years ago, are 'English-ruled and English-led.' I am, etc., E. GREY"

Continuation of previous document as discovered in Foreign Office in London during German occupation in 1921:

"You will intercept this properly to Baron Kato. He will learn from the Japanese Ambassador here the extent and direction of our preparations."

English White Paper, No. 55.
Sir. E. Grey to Sir M. de C. Findlay, British Ambassador to Washington:

"April 22, 1920. You will convey to the Secretary of State the information that His Majesty's Government views with great concern the latest developments in Mexico. For many years English interests in that country have been detrimentally affected, and only the regard of His Majesty's Government for the traditional policy of the United States has enabled us to tolerate the conditions which have prevailed. Whatever may be the decision of the American Government as to the Japanese claims when the interrupted negotiations with that country are resumed, English interests will not permit us to tolerate any further violation of our rights in Mexico. The action of the British Community in Mexico in raising and arming a force for the protection of their lives and properties is something in which His Majesty's Government is not directly concerned, but to which, it feels, the American Government should have no objection. I am, etc., E. GREY."

Dispatches to various American papers:

"Mexico City, May 1, 1920. Japanese troops and colonists are proceeding to occupy their latest concessions, the States of Morelos and Aguascalientes."

Sir E. Grey in Parliament, May 26, 1920:

"The present unfortunate tension between the United States and Japan is a matter of great regret to us. We are the friend to both nations. We can anticipate no difficulty with that great Republic which has sprung of our own people and institutions—that second

England, as we are proud to call it. An unsettled state of affairs in North America would, of course, affect us instantly, but we are taking steps to peaceably guard every English interest. Our transports are nearing Halifax, and the Canadian army is under arms and recruiting. Our new Caribbean fleet is in the waters which it was created to protect. The watchfulness of England, designed to assist the preservation of peace, should give a sense of security to all. I am, etc., E. GREY."

English White Paper, No. 90.

"June 15, 1920. You will communicate to the Secretary of State that our occupation of Progresso in Mexico is designed, as he assumed, to assist in the preservation of peace. It is, of course, temporary. Assure the Secretary of our high appreciation of his understanding of our purposes. I am, etc., E. GREY."

Editorial in New York *Times*, July 22, 1920.

"The decision of the Conference of American Peace Societies to hold mass meetings in all the great cities of the country within the next fortnight is a source of gratification to all true patriots.

The jingo is by no means extinct in America, as the last few days have shown. The only danger that can possibly threaten us is the danger of intemperate excitability. This is clear to all unprejudiced minds now that England has so signally shown her friendship by assembling English troops at Halifax and Hindu regiments at Vancouver, as well as taking steps to protect white interests in Mexico.

"In view of this splendid vindication of our policy of especial friendship for England, it would seem that the irreconcilables might at last be silenced; but unfortunately some of them are trying to represent as a danger this magnificent demonstration of Anglo-Saxon unity. The wise counsel of such men as Mr. Taft, Judge Parker, John Hays Hammond, Dr. Eliot, and Dr. Jordan, delivered from a score of platforms, should silence these agitators.

"The brightest hope kindled by the recent developments is that Japan may yet agree to take the whole matter to The Hague. The refusal of the Mikado's Government to submit the tangled questions–Chinese, Mexican, and Californian–to the International Court has been the most baffling feature of the negotiations." Japanese White Paper, No. 205. Baron Kato, Japanese Minister of

Foreign Affairs, to Count Hioki, Japanese Ambassador at Washington:

"July 12, 1920. You will please communicate to the Honorable Secretary of State that His Imperial Majesty's Government can no longer tolerate the conditions prevailing in Mexico and California, which are now aggravated by the dispatch of an American fleet to the Pacific. His Imperial Majesty's Government must therefore respectfully demand that the American Government within 48 hours from noon of July 13th, recall its fleet, demobilize its troops on the Mexican border, and signify its intentions to promptly satisfy our demands as to Mexico and California. I am, etc., KATO."

English White Paper, No. 132. Sir E. Grey to Sir M. de C. Findlay:

"July 13th, 1920. You will communicate to the Secretary of State that His Majesty's Government would have to view very gravely any act of the American Government which would violate the neutrality of Mexico or of any Central or South American Republic, or cause a disturbance in the Caribbean, or interrupt the freedom of commerce in the Panama Canal, which is essentially a neutral waterway for facilitating the world's commerce. These

things will appeal strongly to public opinion here. I am, etc., E.

GREY."

SIR M. DE C. FINDLAY

"Made English Ambassador to the United States in recognition of his services in

attempting to assassinate Sir Roger Casement."

English White Paper, No. 150. Sir E. Grey to Sir M. de C. Findlay:

"July 16, 1920. You will advise the Secretary of State that the refusal of the American Government to give satisfactory assurances in the matters of the present violations of Mexican, Panamanian, and Colombian neutrality, accomplished by forcible assault on the natural protectors of those countries, and accompanied by atrocities committed by the American invaders, together with the naval occupation of the Panama Canal and the disturbances of the Caribbean, compel His Majesty's Government to take military and naval steps against the United States. You will ask for your passports at once. We have already handed the American Ambassador his passports. I am, etc., E. GREY."

Communication from Lord Kitchener, President of the Consolidated Grand Trunk-Canadian Pacific Railway System, to Premier Asquith. Discovered in London during German occupation in 1921.

Cablegram, July 17, 1921. "Asquith, London: The Canadian Parliament having ratified a declaration of war, our strategic plans will now proceed to execution: the invasion of New York, the capture of Chicago, the march on Pittsburgh, the isolation of the grain States, the expedition up the Mississippi, the blockade of every port and the conquest by our Allies of the Western and Southwestern States. As you have said, no action need be taken against Washington, where we are already as powerful as we could wish. I sail to-day. KITCHENER."

The foregoing selection of documents presents a very different view of the causes of the War of 1920 from that given in the European press during these months. It overflowed with articles justifying the English action on every exalted ground of political morality. The United States was denounced as a despot of the two Americas, deliberately plotting the annexation of its fellow republics; fostering discord and revolution, quarreling with Japan as an excuse for aggression, finally launching a sudden attack on Mexico, Panama, and Colombia.

Uncle Sam was cartooned as the swaggering assassin of liberty, half beast and half bandit, walking through seas of innocent blood to a tyrant's throne. The whole thing was startlingly like the attitude of the American press in 1914 toward Germany and the Kaiser; and why not? Both opinions were made in England, by the same degenerate nation, the same sinister statesmen, the same press system, merely turned against a different victim!

In the next chapter the Japanese-Hindu invasion of Oregon and Washington will be described.

Destroying the Panama Canal and the American Navy

IV

On the 14th of July the Great American Pacific Fleet was slowly passing through the Panama Canal, the administration at last having yielded to public opinion. Ten super dreadnaughts, one first-class battle-cruiser, seven older warships, six submarines, twenty destroyers, four light cruisers, one mine-layer, and sundry colliers, supply ships, and hospital ships; one by one they were stepped up the locks, one by one they entered the deep canyon of Culebra.

The tropic sun was sinking in a sanguine blaze as the great *Pennsylvania* and the historic old *Oregon* reached the narrowed part of the Cut. What happened then has been described to me by an officer of the *Arkansas,* which was next in line. A dreadful stillness seemed suddenly to possess air, a ghastly, dizzy silence, out of which, like a million fiends, there leapt deafening roars of sound; and as if they rushed to a horrid embrace, the two towering walls of the Cut plunged toward each other. In a twinkling the *Pennsylvania* and the *Oregon* were buried beneath countless tons of earth, and all on board found death and their graves in one instant.

The Canal was blocked by a mountain which it would take months to remove–the American Pacific fleet was cut in half. By order of Admiral Black, whose flagship *District of Columbia* led the line toward the Pacific, the ships nearest the scene of the disaster devoted themselves to the vain work of rescue, while the marines of all the other vessels were hurried ashore, on both banks, with orders to spread in a wide circle and capture whatever suspicious characters they could find. Night closed down; some of the companies stumbled about in the jungle through the dark, others encamped and took up the chase in the morning.

Shortly after dawn fifty marines crossed the line between Canal Zone and the Republic of Panama–without knowing it, though they would have done the same had they known–and were fired on from a small native village. Four men dropped, and with an enraged yell their comrades charged. Lithe figures dashed out one by one of the huts and disappeared in the jungle. That hut the marines, after vainly searching, set afire, and unfortunately the blaze spread and consumed the whole village. One woman had accidently been hit by an American bullet, and, unable to move, she died in the flames as the marines passed on. Panama territory was invaded at other points, and another army of marines, fired on at a village where they were requisitioning food, killed two natives, but missed a Japanese who instigated the native resistance and then fled to the jungle.

Not for many days was it discovered how Japanese spies had patiently dug tunnels from the jungle to the brink of the Cut, drilled numerous broad, deep holes, filled them with terrible new Japanese explosive "Banzaiite," and exploded the charges from electrical batteries within Panamanian territory. Not for months was it known that they had brought overland from Salina Cruz, the Eastern terminus of the Tehauntepec Railroad, the oxygen machines, the silent electric drills, the batteries, and the explosives for their deadly work.

With dawn of the 15th came word from the Pacific fortifications of the Canal that they were under bombardment of a powerful Japanese fleet and that the light cruiser *Tacoma,* one of the few American naval vessels in the Pacific, approaching Panama for her expected rendezvous with the Pacific fleet, had been fired on by the Japs and was speeding to the South before three pursuers. At the end of a morning's chase the *Tacoma* reported by wireless that she was shattered and sinking had had run aground on a lonely beach, that her surviving crew was going ashore. For seven days nothing was heard of these fugitives directly, but as we shall see, much was heard indirectly.

The same day it was learned that Japanese fleets and transports were at Manila and Honolulu, and the capture of the Philippines and Hawaii was a matter of their convenience. The effect of these events in the United States can be better imagined than described. Mobs, composed of all classes of citizens, raged through the streets of the larger cities, vainly seeking Japanese victims, and failing to find them, gathered in huge meetings to demand vengeance. Vengeance—but how was it to be had?

The newspaper could only tell the people to look to England. All day on the 15th, all morning on the 16th, the question was asked, "What will England do?" And the answer the newspapers gave was "Trust England!" Did not the English have a fleet at Vera Cruz, another at Jamaica? Were there not Hindus at Vancouver, English at Halifax, Canadians mobilized at Montreal?

The papers on the morning of the 16th barely mentioned that the presidents of Panama, Colombia, and Mexico had appealed to England against the violation of their "neutrality," in the first instance by the marines from the fleet, in the second case by the crew of the *Tacoma*, who had landed on Colombian territory and were alleged to have committed terrible atrocities on the helpless natives, and in the third instance by the Texas Rangers. For, on the 15th, a report had come across the border that a great force of allied Japanese and Mexicans, proceeding North on the National railroad of Mexico, had reached Monterey. Whereupon two companies of

Texas Rangers, stationed on the border by the Governor against the request of the State Department, crossed the Rio Grande with a whoop, not knowing where they would go or what they could do, but determined, at last, after seven years of waiting to "go for the greasers!"

The old leaders of discord in Mexico—Villa, Zapata, Carranza, Felix Diaz, and the grim Huerta—had long since killed each other off, but there was no lack of lesser bandits to carry on the chief business of the country. Particularly the shrewd, unscrupulous Pasqual Orozco, a veteran of all factions, a leader who always played safe, had risen in these degenerate days, and had held Mexico City for more than a year. It was an open secret to all the world that he was propped in power by the unofficial support of the Japanese and English Governments. The former dealt with him through Viscount Isuki, Resident chairman of the Consolidated Japanese Company of Mexico; the latter through Major Hawkes, Commander of the Guard of the British Community—the Community being composed of all English exploiters in Mexico, the Guard of about 1,000 adventurers, bandits and cutthroats, white and Mexican.

It was afterward shown that English and Japanese diplomacy had succeeded in getting control of the ruling cliques of Panama and Colombia. In the form case it was bribery; in the latter, threats. The ruling powers of Colombia were told quite frankly that England and Japan would shortly be in possession of Panama and the Canal, and that Colombia's security depended on her aid in this plot.

The Colombian authorities communicated this to the American State Department, where they were begged to hush and never breathe a word about it. Neither the State Department nor the Colombian Government ever did breathe a word about it, but the Latin-American statesmen, overwhelmed with disgust at the spectacle of a great nation afraid to protest against English and Japanese aggression, capitulated to the Allies. So it came about that the protests of all three Latin-American Republics against the violation of their neutrality and the commission of atrocities by American forces reached London on late July 15th. It reminds one forcibly of the prearranged stage-play of ex-King Albert, whom England had so securely in her grip through her power to take or leave his enormous rubber properties!

The afternoon of the 16th came, and for the first time in mad weeks the newspapers in the chief cities of America failed to send out extra after extra. There was a sudden hush in the busy avenues where the newsboys were wont to herald every development, every rumor. The bulletin boards were washed bare. People began to winder, and questioned each other in tones that betrayed a premonition of something unprecedented.

Suddenly the groups of newsboys gathered about the offices received their awaited bundles, the wagons and automobiles were loaded and rushed off, and through street after street, in a thousand cities of America, the staggering, incredible news was spread:

ENGLAND DECLARES WAR ON THE UNITED STATES!

The Ring of Iron Tightens

V

The situation of the United States after the Sixteenth of July, 1920, was strikingly like that of Germany after the First of August, 1914. In each case a Ring or Iron, carefully forged around the intended victim by English intrigue, began to strangle that victim. In each case, foes were pouring over every border while superior naval forces closed the ways overseas. In each case the hordes of every color that humanity has assumed were marshalled against a white race and against white men's homes. There the comparison ceased.

In 1914, the German people, having placed patriotism above politics and the Nation about business, having schooled themselves to act as one in National necessity, having learned in their great democratic army to think and fight, having developed their Navy scientifically, were able to instantly hold off their foes and to carry the battle safely beyond they own borders.

In 1920, the American people, having preferred business and politics to patriotism and Nationalism, having been only too ready to believe the easy doctrines of the Pacifists–who, strangely enough, were always Anglophiles or Anglomaniacs!–beheld the hosts of the foe possessing their soil, their cities, North, East, South, and West, and had nothing at hand with which to resist them. The passionate attempts of individuals and little groups to stay the invaders met with the prompt punishment which the Law of War decrees against sniping.

The full rigors of the catastrophe were brought home first to the people of the State of Washington. All the years of speculation about a Japanese war had failed to warn Pacific Coast Americans that danger really threatened from the North. There were, on the 12th of July, two divisions of Hindu troops at Vancouver. That day five English transports sailed up the Strait of Juan de Fuca bearing nearly another division, to the great satisfaction of the American people.

At the same time, three hundred miles to the North, twenty big steamers of the Nippon Yusen Kaisha, one of the great Japanese steamship lines which are heavily subsidized in order that their great vessels, which are specially designed for the purpose, may be quickly turned into transports, entered Queen Charlotte Sound, North of Vancouver Island, and slowly steamed toward Nanaimo, opposite Vancouver, bearing to anchorage there on the 13th and 14th, sixty thousand warriors of Japan with full equipment. The news was not heralded to the people of the United States, and indeed on the evening of the 12th British Columbia was put under martial law, and no news was permitted to leak out. This was considered by the American people as another step for their protection!

The news of the Japanese ultimatum reached the Coast States

on the afternoon of the 12th, and the people, who had exhibited marvelous restraint therefore, spontaneously began a Jap hunt. Strange to relate, not a Jap was to be found! Silently, unnoticed, they had left the cities; subtly, under guise of harmless picnic parties or by way of paying friendly visits to distance relatives, they had deserted their farms. The people were amazed, but it took days to gather sufficient threads of information to discover that the whole Japanese population of the Pacific Coast had either fled to Canada or swiftly concentrated in three prepared strategic positions in the mountains—three natural fortresses, now guarded by thousands of Japanese, every man of them a trained soldier, a reservist for the Empire! The women and children were adequately sheltered, and every approach was dominated machine guns and rifles.

The Japanese of Washington had fled to Canada; those of Oregon and Northern California had entrenched on a spur of Mr. Shasta; those of the Sacramento Valley and the regions around San Francisco had chosen a series of caves in the Mt. Diablo range, on the border of Monterey and Fresno counties; those of South California were discovered in a glen at the southern edge of Santa

Anna Mountains, in Riverside County. The positions had been selected with great skill, having regard to accessibility from nearby railroads and through river valleys, and were in the highest degree defensible, as the posses which first came upon them discovered to their cost.

On the 16th the Governor of the State was apprised of the situation, and the orders to the State Militia to attack these "alien fortresses in the heart of fair California" were before him for his signature, when the more startling news of the English declaration stayed his pen. With the sanction of the authorities, however, volunteer companies, stern ne and venturesome youths, entered upon regular sieges of Japanese positions. And the Japanese—nearly twelve thousand trained warriors, amply provisioned, impregnably stationed—easily fought them off and calmly awaited the march of their armies from North and South.

At midnight of July 16th a church bell in the prosperous little city of Bellingham, Washington, startled the sleeping citizens with hysteric tolling. They flocked to the windows, to the streets. And there the incredible rumor ran that the city was in the hands of the enemy! The intrepid and the curious hastened back to the railroad, and there, quietly but unmistakably ordering them back, they came upon long companies of little men in uniform, with rifles and fixed bayonets; and beyond, over the iron rails there rolled train after train, darkened, a silence save for the plaintive ring of rails under heavy, steady, slow-moving wheels, trains filled with more little men with rifles and bayonets, and with all the equipment of an army. All night they rolled on, to the South, over the rails of the Great Northern; when other trains were overtaken or met going North, the crews were overpowered and the cars and engines added to the rolling stock of the invaders. In the morning the head of the column was proceeding down the Eastern shore of Lake Washington, in back of Seattle.

There was no need of military action against Seattle. The proud metropolis of the Northwest awoke to look into the grey guns of eight Japanese cruisers in Elliott Bay. Guided by officers who had often brought the merchant liners of Japan through the channels of Puget Sound, they had left their berths off Victoria, Vancouver Island, where they had arrived on the 15th, and had slid through the dark, past the small and hastily planted minefield in Admiralty Inlet. Seattle was at their mercy.

THE CAPTURE OF SEATTLE

"Desperate citizens were making their...defense of their city."

A flotilla of small boats, in one of which was a captain bearing a demand of the surrender of the city and a ransom of $20,000,000 approached the wharves. A revolver cracked, then another, then perhaps dozen. Desperate citizens were making their instinctive, tragic defense of their city. A sailor threw up his hands and toppled over, then an officer. The boats were suddenly swung around; sharp staccato orders were given, and little squads of marines in the sterns raised their rifles and swept the wharves with deadly fire. A dozen men fell; the unarmed spectators fled with cries of horror and rage; but a few men with revolvers crouched behind bales and continued to snipe the Japs as they rowed swiftly forward.

Then a gasp, a cry of horror, rose from everyone who could see the ships; for a wisp of smoke curled from one of the eight-inch guns of the *Kasuga*, the deep bark of artillery sounded, and far off, apparently in a distant residential section, an explosion, which consequence could only be guessed at with horror, told that the shell had struck home. Before the terrified city had caught its breath, a roar, louder and fiercer than before, filled the air, as the seven six-inch guns in the port barbettes of the *Nisshin* fired in unison; each shell found its mark in a difference warehouse in the shipping district, and besides scores of casualties within buildings, falling walls and flying masonry killed and injured two dozen people. It was afterward learned that the victims of the eight-inch shell were a mother and her two children, one of whom was at her breast when the horrible explosion tore them to bloody fragments.

As the cries of agony and despair arose following the volley, the Mayor of the City arrived at the wharves in an automobile, and, jumping out, waved a white pillow-case, which he had snatched as he left his home. There was no more firing of big guns or little; the boats drew near, a Captain leapt out and presented the demand for surrender, and the Mayor in a scarcely audible voice submitted. How the collection of the ransom and the looting of the city of all of its stores of food, coal, and oil were carried out; how these things were loaded on every serviceable coastline American craft in the harbor and sent to Tacoma, and how the vessels were then declared forfeit and sent to British Columbia, need not detain us. Seattle was looted thoroughly–that is the main fact.

The next chapter will describe Funston's victory at Spokane; and the conquest of Texas.

The Greaser Rules Texas

VI

The Texas Rangers who crossed the Rio Grande at Laredo on July 15th reached the railroad line at Palo Blanco ten days later, much the worse for hunger and third, only to learn that a great force had already invaded their state. So they traveled back to Texas, losing ten dead and twenty-six wounded on the way. A bigger game was afoot than they were prepared to play, and they symbolized all America in that.

At Brownsville, Texas, near the mouth of the Rio Grande, there were stationed a brigade of United States infantry, a regiment of cavalry, and a regiment of light field artillery, mustered to nearly war strength, altogether about 7,500 men, commanded by Major-General Barry. Orozco ostentatiously declared war on the United States on the 17th of July, an example followed by the other Mexican chiefs successively, and on the 18th American troops occupied Matamoras. Sniping occurred, and a part of the town had to be shelled, with the result that a number of women and children as well as men fell before the blind vengeance of the guns. War is much the same everywhere, given the same conditions! I have seen English papers of that time giving lurid accounts of the "slaughter of innocents" by the American "barbarians!"

On the 19th the head of the approaching Japanese-Mexican army was reported at Reynosa, sixty miles away on the railroad line. The American army, unappalled by the prospect of being greatly outnumbered, was eager to give battle, and had made good defensive preparations; but the pleasure was denied them for the time being, for on the evening of the 20th it was learned that the enemy had crossed the Rio Grande near Reynosa and were advancing along the line of the branch railroad toward Harlingen, Texas, in the rear of the American position. The evacuation of Matamoras and Brownsville instantly became imperative, and only quick work and a stubborn defense near Harlingen prevented the retreat being cut.

A defense was undertaken at Kingsville, 150 miles north of the Rio Grande, where the left flank of the American force was protected by an inlet of the Gulf. The action resulted in delaying the Allied advance a few hours, and the defenders lost 700 men before they retreated at dusk under shrapnel fire which momentarily increased in volume as more and more guns were brought up.

Trains of volunteer wreckers had come down the line and from this point they tore up large sections of track all the way to Houston. And the invaders rolled on at leisure, for the work of raiding and looting was their chief business. The main forces followed the line of the Southern Pacific, rebuilding as they went, bringing their sustenance with them, abandoning communications. But the mounted bandits of Mexico overrode and devastated all the

Gulf country, looting and destroying cotton plantations, oil wells, stock farms, and huge scientific farms with their varied wealth.

Texas will never forget the horror and the shame of that raid. From many an isolated farm and plantation the men, women, and children had been unable to fleet. Many a tale of horror has survived that inundation by the grinning, cruel, lustful "Greasers"; many a tale of desperate defense by the brave men of the ranches, ending in death for them and worse than death for the women and children they vainly died for. The desperate defenses made by the regulars and the militia of Texas, Louisiana, Mississippi, and Arkansas at Wharton and behind the Brazos River need not detain us, as they did not detain the invaders. They told the same story, at first so astounding, but now so tragically familiar to the American people; the unprepared overwhelmed by the prepared; the superior race helpless before the inferior; bravery counting for naught; an army with 40 field pieces overwhelmed by one of 250; an unguarded treasure land at the mercy of looters; the inevitable price of Pacifism; the sure reward of Anglophilisim.

On the 25th of August, Houston surrendered; on the 26th, Galveston. In the former city sniping occurred, and in retaliation all public buildings were destroyed. At Galveston and at Port

Arthur vast stores of cotton and oil were captured; the country for

two hundred miles from the coast ravaged; by the 20th of

September the Japanese and Mexicans were before New Orleans,

which already for many days had cowered under the guns of

English and French cruisers. How France had been brought into

line with the international assassins we shall see presently.

The few hundred men composing the militia of Arizona and

New Mexico, together with Rangers and a few regular

infantrymen, were kept busy during these months pursuing the

bands of Mexican raiders who slipped over the border, here, there

and everywhere, murdering, ravishing, and looting. The rest of the

regular troops on the border, about 3,000 men of all arms

(deducting the 7,500 who had retreated from Brownsville, and

were now reduced to less than 4,000), had been sent to California.

The apprehension in which Tacoma passed the 17th of July

needs no vivid imagination to picture it. Women and children were

hurried out of the city on every possible line of road, while the men

debated whether or not to defend the city. The leaders of all walks

of life decided to make the inevitable submission at once, to avoid disaster; but bands of hotheaded men began to assemble along the railroad, and to build barricades in the steep hilly streets. A section of track was torn up, but before the afternoon waned into evening, the head of the invaders' first train appeared, while about the same time, three cruisers entered Commencement Bay and held the city under their guns.

The first rifle shots that pattered against the armored engine of the oncoming train were answered instantly by swift volleys poured from little port-holes of the first car, which was likewise heavily armored, while, to the amazement of the foolish defenders, the second car opened upon their hidden positions with storms of shrapnel, and from the third two guns of large caliber sent huge shells whistling towards the city, there to crash with terrible force among homes and churches and schools. The defenders fled.

No shots were fired at the sailors and marines who came to receive the surrender of the city, and fortunately the men behind the barricades thought better of their intention of resisting, so that Tacoma escaped further damage. A ransom of $15,000,000 was collected during the next two days, and all seizable foodstuffs and stores of military value were added to those brought from Seattle, as the long trains of the invaders moved southward again on the 18th.

The cruisers commanding Seattle had meanwhile been attacked by two destroyers which dashed out of the Navy Yard at Bremerton across the Sound; but before the intrepid little craft could get within torpedo range they were overwhelmed and sunk by gun-fire.

Nobody seemed to think of tearing up the railroad tracks before the swift advance of the invaders through the rest of West Washington, and on the evening of the 21st, having brushed aside the opposition of a battalion of Oregon militia at the crossing of the Columbia River, they entered Portland. The citizens noticed that there were Hindus among the invaders, though the greater part of the force was Japanese. That they were a huge host was made evident by the next moves.

The heavily guarded rail communications with British Columbia were abandoned down to Tacoma, after every town and village on the way had been looted of all foodstuffs and fuel, every bank robbed, every piece of rolling stock sent Southward. Only Seattle and Tacoma retained garrisons of the foe, while water communication with Canada was commanded by Japanese cruisers. A Japanese base was also established by marines from cruisers which appeared off Astoria, at the mouth of the Columbia, and kept the line of that river to Portland open by threatening to punish any interference with the railroad lines or any opposition to their use of the river by a bombardment of every town and village along the river. The line from Tacoma to Portland was also garrisoned.

The invaders now had a host at Portland sufficient to detach one army which struck swiftly up the Columbia, while another continued to penetrate to the South. Of the latter it is sufficient to record that despite the destruction of the railroads in many places, in twenty days it had blazed a path of ruin, robbery, and rape through the rich country of Western Oregon to the borders of California. Sniping occurred, of course, and just after the second instance of it, all restrain was removed by Japanese commanders–and by the English Brigadier-General who accompanied them in a subordinate capacity–and the lust and bloodlust of the Orientals, waxing ever greater the more it found to feed on, devoted to shame every woman and girl who had been unable to escape, and to death every man, and to the flames every house and other property that could not be removed.

The expedition that struck up the Columbia found the railroad intact for two hundred miles, till on the 28th the junction of the Lewis Fork or Snake River with the Columbia was reached. There a force of 2,000 Washington Militia, with one battery of mountain guns, 3,500 volunteers from Eastern Washington, and 3,000 miners from the Coeur d'Alene district of Idaho–fighting Irishmen–determined to offer resistance despite the usual threats of punishment for "civilian resistance." They blew up the bridges and entrenched on the hills in the bend of the rivers, but the enemy, who mustered at least two divisions and certain additional regiments, or about 50,000 men–minus a few left to guard the line–promptly detached two raiding parties, up the fertile Yakima and Walla-Walla valleys, and while they looted, robbed, and burned, and returned laden with stores of fruit, vegetables, and fodder, the main force calmly shot the defenders out of their trenches with heavy artillery, and on the 4th of August resumed their march on Spokane and Idaho.

That march was grimly opposed every step of the way by the

little army of volunteers, who were commanded by General Funston, and the ruin which the invaders spread with fire and shell was paid for with losses of nearly 8,000 men before the 24th of August found them forty miles from Spokane and face to face with a new opposition.

Beyond the town of Sprague there is a district of hills and lakes. The reconnaissances made by the Japanese cavalry and aeroplanes developed a considerable force of Americans cleverly disposed on this excellent defensive ground. Funston had now, in fact, besides the 3,000 survivors of the little force which had been delaying the Japanese advance, two infantry regiments and two mountain batteries, together numbering something less than 4,000 men, from the Boise Barracks, Idaho; Fort Issoula, Montana; and Fort D.A. Russell, Wyoming; about 5,000 Washington, Montana, and Idaho militia, with two mountain batteries; and about 10,000 volunteers, chiefly miners, lumbermen, and sheep rangers.

With characteristic Japanese care and leisureliness, the enemy set about shooting them out of their positions with heavy artillery, beginning on the 27th of August. But on the 1st of September a sortie by the American forces, carried out with a skill and desperate courage that overwhelmed the Orientals, and succeeded in disabling or destroying most of their big guns. The Japanese commander, General Naganuma, then launched a general attack. He did not dare to outflank the Americans by going around the hills, for that would have left his own flank and communications exposed.

Probably 10,000 of the enemy troops had been lost along the lines of communication, and deducting these and their losses, they must have brought into battle on the 4th of September about 29,000 men. Opposed to them the defenders mustered now about 20,000. The result of the assault was that the invaders were trapped amid the lakes and glens, and by night were in full retreat, leaving over 4,000 dead and wounded and about 5,300 prisoners.

The victory of Spokane was a tonic to the country, and yet at what price had it been won! What a commentary on American politics, American diplomacy, American pacifism were those hundreds of blackened country, depopulated, with thousands of homes in ashes; those valleys once the marvel of the world for fertility, now stripped too bare to give sustenance to a crow! What a price in dead and wounded men and violated women had been paid for that curious blindness to Japanese truculence and English treachery!

THE AMERICANS UNPREPARED BUT BRAVE

"The march was opposed every step by General Funston."

The Allied troops withdrew from Oregon, having such huge supplies and stores in their thousands of cars that they could cut loose from their base and roll on to establish another from which they could conduct from their big job of raiding and looting California.

The next chapter will describe the collapse of the American forces in the West and the subjugation of the white race.

The Subjugation of the White Man

VII

n the 15th of July, a Japanese squadron appeared off San Diego, California. Two older American cruisers and three destroyers stationed there attempted to approach within torpedoing distance of the enemy that night, but were driven off by a hail of shells. Daily, thereafter, the cruisers of the Island Empire paraded slowly up and down the horizon.

On the morning of the 23rd the American destroyers dashed out at sunrise, and, approaching the enemy in swift zigzag courses, endeavored to get within striking distance while the brilliant morning sun shone in the eyes of the Japanese gun-captains and glinted dazzlingly on the choppy waves. The heroic effort seemed about to succeed as the shots from the cruisers splashed vainly in the opal waters; but just as the foremost destroyer, the *O'Brien*, was about to discharge its torpedo, a ten-inch shell struck her fairly between the funnels. There was one terrific explosion, a momentary phantasmagoria of hurtling steel, geysering water, hissing steam and pale flame, and the waters closed over wrecked vessel and mangled men. The new *Evans*, one of the latest and most powerful of American torpedo craft, laboring with engine-trouble, was behind the *O'Brien;* and, discharging a torpedo at an impossible range, she turned with the third destroyer and sped back to shelter pursued by volleys of shot.

That night, and for seven days thereafter, small steamers landed Japanese from South America—farmers there, but trained reservists—at a lonely place on the coast, near Escondido Junction, thirty-five miles north of San Diego. For some days the beautiful city had heard of forces of Japanese and Mexicans hovering near the borders of Lower California. Cavalry scouts from the United States Military Reservation on Point Loma had been sent out, and on the 24th, coincident with the news of the landing of forces on the Coast, they reported that about half a division of Japanese infantry had crossed the border twenty miles away.

A panicky exodus of women, children, the aged, and the timid began at once, over the line of railroad that did not lead directly toward the invading forces—the San Diego and Southeastern, a little road leading barely forty miles into the mountains! Even this precarious haven was not reached by many of the refugees, for on the 26th a force of 6,000 mounted Mexicans, who had come around the San Ysidro Mountains and down the Sweetwater Valley, descended upon the towns along that route. Savages of the cruelest type, utterly without restraint, they conducted warfare as the Redskins of centuries before had conducted it, and the fate met by all the men, women, and children they came upon added a fresh weight of horror to the terrible burden being laid upon the desperate defenders of the Pacific Coast.

On the 27th the Japanese squadron was reinforced by the great superdreadnought *Fuso*, and approached within thirteen miles of

Point Loma. The military post at this point was in process of being made into a first-class coast defense fortress after the leisurely fashion followed by Congress in accordance with the sacred custom of annual appropriations. Three twelve-inch mortars and one sixteen-inch disappearing rifle were in place, inadequately masked, insufficiently supplied with ammunition, manned by not over one-half the proper force.

At 11 A.M. a fleet of eight hydro-aeroplanes rose from the Japanese ships, and soon they were circling over the fortifications and dropping little balls of soot and little showers of tinsel, to indicate the gunners of the squadron the location of the coastal defenses. At 11:20 the sixteen-inch gun opened fire on the attackers, and in a moment the action was general. Never in the history of modern warfare has a fleet succeeded in overcoming up-to-date coastal defenses; but here the battle was between four unmasked guns, rather than a fortress, and a powerful naval force.

Before 12 o'clock one of the mortars was wrecked by a shot from the *Fuso.* A few minutes later a shot from the sixteen-inch gun found a fair, true mark amidships of the old battleship *Suo,* which retired with a heavy list. A moment later, as the sixteen-inch gun rose again, the great broadside of the *Fuso,* directed by the airmen, found its mark; six 14-inch shells, striking in a little circle, fairly hurled the coast defender and its huge steel carriage into the air, and over the broad earth-covered wall of the fort. The tremendous shock wrenched one of the remaining mortars loose, while flying fragments killed or wounded several of the crew of the other. Nevertheless, the last mortar continued firing, scoring a minor hit on the cruiser *Yakamo,* till the terrible shower of metal at last put gun and gun-crew out of action.

At 12:45, immediately after two cruisers had turned their guns on the cities of Coronado and San Diego, the commander of the coast defense and mobile defenses at Point Lima ran up the white flag to avoid useless destruction of life and property. The mobile forces, numbering about 5,000 regulars, of whom 3,000 had come from the Mexican border a few days before, with 1,000 militia and about 2,000 volunteers, could have broken through the encircling forces of Japanese and Mexicans, but the Japanese commander, Admiral Kamaya, insisted on their surrender under the threat of destroying not only Coronado and San Diego, but every town on the coast. Two cruisers and destroyers were also surrendered. On the 30th, 2,000 marines were landed to guard the environs of San Diego, while most of the fleet moved northward, and the Japanese troops and their savage allied turned towards Los Angeles.

SAN DIEGO UNDER ORIENTAL EYES

"A fleet of eight hydro-aeroplanes rose from the Japanese ships."

Since the 15th of July, Japanese fleets had been blockading San Francisco and the coasts of Los Angeles and Orange Counties.

The Allied Japanese and Mexican troops advanced toward the North, close to the coast, sending out raiding parties in every direction, levying tribute on towns where any inhabitants awaited their coming, robbing any bank where money had been left, and occasionally committing outrages on women, though the Japanese commander restrained all but the most lawless Mexicans. There were troops, regular and militia, at San Francisco, none at Los Angeles; and so terror-stricken were the people of the city by the Golden Gate and those of the northern part of the State, that no help could be sent to the metropolis of the Southwest and the prosperous, beautiful section around it.

The advancing Allies were joined by the 5,000 Japanese reservists, who had been entrenched in the Santa Ana Mountains, and approached Tustin, thirty-five miles from Los Angeles, 29,000 strong. At this point, on the outer circumference of a circle that could be drawn to include Los Angeles and the thickly settled district of beautiful suburbs closely connected with it by numerous rail and trolley lines, one company of militia and 2,000 old volunteers threw themselves furiously on the flank of the Allied advance guard. That was on August 12th. The gallant Americans inflicted a loss of over 500 on the invaders, but were in the end killed, wounded, or captured to the last man.

The next two weeks were veritable Hell and Chaos to all in that district, once so proud of its wealth, its beauty, its newest Americanism. Far and wide the raiders carried unrestrained outrage and destruction, and many thousands who were unable to escape on the gorged and crowded railroads paid with death, shame, or lingering concentration camps for the "atrocity" of that attack by uninformed patriots on the ravagers of their country.

On the 20th of August, Los Angeles itself was entered in force—the invaders had already scoured the country to the North as well as to the South of it—and in a broad plaza near the hearty of the city, 400 Americans who had been made captives as Tustin were assembled. Lots were drawn; 200 were marked for death. Some odd thousands of the city's population had been driven hither to witness the terrible deed now perpetrated. In batches of ten the helpless victims were lined against a wall, and ten by ten they were murdered by impassive Japanese, while the Mexicans danced and shouted with delight, and the assembled citizens shuddered in a horror unbroken by sound, a horror that left many a man broken in nerve and sent many a woman insane. Thus were the patriots, who sprang to arms in the hour of their country's need, according to the gospel of the Pacifists, rewarded.

Meanwhile, in the North, the Japanese and Hindu Allies had crossed the line from Oregon, nearly 50,000 strong. Advancing by rail, they approached Deadwood on August 15th. They were in constant wireless touch with the 3,000 reservists entrenched at the foot of Mt. Shasta, and these now made a sally, fighting their way through the encircling line of volunteer besiegers. On the 16th they joined the advancing host, while the Americans retreated, tearing up the railroad, which at this point enters the mountains, and offered ineffectual guerrilla resistance.

By August 30th the invaders had reached Redding, at the head of the Sacramento Valley. They left about 8,000 troops along the lines of communications. Advancing nearly 44,000 strong, in fifteen days they reached the town of Glen. There they established headquarters and divided into numerous raiding parties. City, town, farm, and mine throughout Glenn, Colusa, Yolo, Butte, Sutter, Placer, Nevada, Yuba, Sierra, and Plumas Counties saw these yellow men descend upon them like apparitions of an incredible dream, like fiends and discredited fable; city, town, farm, and mine were theirs, and vengeance was theirs wherever stern Americans, scornful of numbers, careless of consequences, maddened beyond endurance, dared to resist them. They returned to Glenn laden with wealth and spoils.

On September 23rd, 17,000 troops, who had retreated from Spokane, joined the forces at this point, the communication guards were called in, the line abandoned as far as Redding, and the irresistible host—minus 2,000 lost on raids—67,000 strong, rolled on toward Sacramento. They entered the Capital of California on October 2nd, and again they halted their advance while they raided Sacramento, Solano, Ambador, Calvers, and Joaquin Counties. Stockton was captured on October 8th, and looted, and the lines began the next day to draw towards San Francisco.

There were stationed, at the beginning of the war, three regiments of infantry at Presidio, and one regiment of cavalry at Monterey; Fort Barry was manned by an insufficient number of coast artillerymen. Following the President's order for mobilization on July 16th, strenuous efforts were made to fill all regiments to their official war strength, and by the first of October this had been approximately done, and another regiment had been recruited and drilled as well as could be. The cavalry from Monterey had been keeping in touch with the Japanese-Mexican force advancing from the South. Practically the whole of the California militia, excepting those whose capture at San Diego, we have noted, had been concentrated near San Francisco.

On October 8th there were something over 7,200 regular infantrymen, about 1,000 surviving cavalrymen, 4,000 militia, including one battery of field artillery, and 8,000 volunteers, part of them acting as field artillery with some guns supplied by the Government arsenal, the rest not all armed alike. The volunteers had contrived a sort of uniform, and all of them were enrolled under the Volunteer Law, the passage and nature of which we shall consider in a following chapter. Of the numerous bands of volunteers, whose exploits I have already chronicled, some had been volunteers in this legal sense, some had not. It was expected that those officially enrolled under the Volunteer Law would be considered by the enemy, whose participation in fighting would not be an excuse for reprisals, and in fact where only volunteers in this legal sense were employed, the enemy generally did accept them as regular and legitimate military.

Thus some 20,000 troops were in the trenches before San Francisco; more could not be mustered because there was abundant need elsewhere for regulars and militia; while no more than 8,000 volunteers could be armed, uniformed, and drilled at this place and time. Opposed to this force were about 65,000 Japanese and Hindus approaching from the North and West minus, perhaps, 10,000 guarding the communications, nearly 28,000 Japanese and Mexicans, fresh from the conquest of San Diego, Los Angeles, and the country thence northward, plus about 4,000 California Japs from the third of their fortresses, in the Diablo Range; altogether about 87,000 yellow, red, and brown men. But this was not all.

For Russia, by means which we shall see, had been brought into this war against her "traditional friend," and on September 1st, 40,000 Russians and 10,000 Japanese had landed, under the unnecessary protection of two small cruisers, at Fort Bragg, about 150 miles from the Golden Gate by way of the Northwestern Pacific Railroad, the ominously named Russian River, and the most populous parts of Mendocino, Sonoma, and Marin counties. Advancing slowly, they wrote another page of the now familiar story; random, bank robbery, requisition of everything edible, looting, swift reprisal when fired on by citizens, nameless outrages against women and girls who could not escape. By October 2nd they had drawn their lines across Marin County from San Pablo Bay to Drake Bay and were putting heavy siege artillery in place to fire on Fort Barry.

The big guns and mortars at Fort Barry had for ten weeks held at bay a great Japanese fleet, and had again proved that properly constructed coast defenses, when armed with guns of the highest possible caliber, are impregnable to attack from the sea. To be sure, one of the big seventeen-inch guns had been put out of action, and several mortars had been struck, but the score had been more than evened by the serious damage inflicted on the *Fuso*, one of whose forward turrets was knocked clean into the sea, and by the sinking of the battle cruiser *Kongo*, with her eight 14-inch guns.

The Japanese, however, had merely fired enough to keep the force at Fort Barry always busy, always worried; they had not attempted to shell the city, which they could have probably done with the most destructive effect had they been willing to risk a ship or two. For Fort Barry alone could not have stopped them; part of that task belonged to the Navy; and there was the Pacific fleet thousands of miles away, half of it near the Atlantic end of the Canal, half near the Pacific, with a great Japanese fleet guarding Panama, and a huge British fleet off Colon.

San Francisco cried loud for the ships at the Pacific end to make a dash; but the Naval Board of Strategy understood that even if some of them miraculously escaped the new Rulers of the Pacific, their arrival in San Francisco Bay would only have aggravated the situation by drawing the fire of the enemy, both ashore and afloat, directly upon the teeming city, with the loss of innocent lives as the chief result. No, Japanese treachery and the infinitely greater treachery of England, and her whelp, Canada, had made the performance of the proper function of the Navy impossible.

There were two submarines of recent type, capable and dangerous craft, at the Mare Island Navy Yard when the blockade began. In the usual course of American political control of national defense, they had an equipment of six torpedoes apiece, and no facilities for making more existed at Mare Island. In the first few days and nights of the blockade they went out seeking victims

among the yellowmen's blockaders. The Japanese were
maintaining the closest watch, however, knowing that those two
underwater dangers lurked near, and always they were detected,
while they miraculously escaped the strenuous efforts of the fleet
to sink them, they had eventually used their six torpedoes apiece in
vain shots at impossible distances. So San Francisco was invested
by land and sea. Thousands of citizens had fled before the line
through Sacramento was closed; few dared or could afford to take
the long route South through Fresno and Kern and up through the
Desert to Salt Lake City. The Southern Pacific had given free
transportation by the first route while it was open, but refused to
over the long way, and there was no way to compel it.

Meanwhile, many more thousands than had gone out had
come in—frightened, ruined refugees from every direction; some
bereaved of every dear one. For ten weeks no food, nothing had
come through the Golden Gate; for several weeks little had come
any other way. Now nothing could come.

The great city lifted up its hands in supplication to God, for help there was none from any other quarter.

THE PATRIOTS OF LOS ANGELES

"Two hundred were marked for death."

They had been told to rely on England, but England was cutting their throats too; they have been told to rely on the might of a million freemen who would spring to arms if the

Administration's sacred peace were broken; but they had seen misery and cruelty unspeakable follow as a swift punishment on the freeman and his wife and children when he sprang to arms. The people of San Francisco cursed the prophets of pacifism; but where Dr. Jordan was no one knew, certainly not here amid the misery that the teachings of himself and his fellows had brought upon his California.

On October 9th fighting began on every side of San Francisco. General Crozier, commanding the defense, was supported by every man of his little army in the determination to inflict what punishment they could upon the treacherous ravagers of the land. A fierce attack by two brigades of infantry and a regiment of cavalry was launched at the left of the Russo-Japanese line, back of San Rafael. The enemy at this point was thrown into confusion, and the regulars, militia, and volunteers vied with each other in racing to the position reported by air-scouts as occupied by big siege howitzers being emplaced for the reduction of Fort Barry. But the invaders had not neglected to protect their big guns with several batteries of field artillery. These were trained on the attackers as they crowded into the little valley behind the village of

Ross or clambered over the hill-sides. Showers of shrapnel bullets and fragments of shell descended like summer rain. German infantry could not have stood it; the hastily drilled, inexperienced Americans could not.

Toward dusk that day twelve American aeroplanes rose and set after the air fleet of the enemy. Only five of these were military machines, the rest were privately owned by San Franciscans, and were manned by their owners, each of whom was accompanied by another young scion of the first families, armed with a rifle. The battle under the clouds was visible for some time after dusk had settled in the valleys, as the rays of the setting sun lingered in the upper air. First blood was scored by an American machine, as a Japanese bird-man was shot through the head and losing control, plunged to earth. Ere long, however, the Americans had been lured within range of the aeroplane guns of the enemy, and as they fired from below, the Japanese and Russian military machines, each armed with a machine gun, turned and became the pursuers. Seven of the American craft returned.

During October 10th the liens of the Japanese-Mexican army drew so close that the greater part of the mobile force had to be sent to the trenches which had been constructed in a broad arc about ten miles beyond Berkley, Oakland, and Alameda. They were good trenches, but the line of defenders in them was, as the army officers knew, ridiculously, pitiably thin. The field artillery was posted behind them on Shell Ridge and Alamo Ridge. The guns opened fire as the enemy's advance column came within range and halted it. But the air-scouts could see column after column, regiment after regiment, steadily rolling forward. Meanwhile, the Mexican horsemen were making progress up San Mateo County, where a little, determined force of volunteers, without trenches, were opposing them from the hills.

Then, at about three o'clock in the afternoon, the field artillery ammunition gave out. The enemy airmen detected the fact. The non-militaristic policy of the United States was vindicated again! After that the invading hosts simply rolled on, careless of the slight damage inflicted by scattering rifle-fire; and before dark, the defenders, broken in nerve at the spectacle of this relentless advance and their impotence to halt it, fled from the trenches. At dawn the morning shells began to burst in Oakland.

Meanwhile, most of the guns of Fort Barry had been destroyed or displaced by the fire of the howitzers, and many of the coast artillery-men, who were now its sole defenders, had been killed or wounded. At midnight a sudden flare of rockets outside the walls lit up with a lurid glare the terrifying spectacle of hundreds, thousands, of Japanese, scaling the walls, bursting through the gates. Fort Barry was theirs. In the morning, the Japanese fleet rode safely in the Golden Gate.

On October 12, 1920, all California lay prostrate between an alien foe; before those two alien foes long had threatened, one the despised foe of Mexico, the other the feared foe Japan; and before foes who had not threatened, but had struck, treacherously, during the very speeches of friendship—England, Canada, and Russia.

But California's humiliation was far from complete. The invasion had only begun. Between October 1st and November 15th, the ships of the *Nippon Yusen Kaisha,* the *Osaka Shosken Kaisha,* and the *Toyo Kisen Kaisha*, 150 steamers, some of them very large and specially adapted for military transportation together with English and Russian ships, brought more than 250,000 Japanese and nearly 50,000 Russians to California and Mexico. During that time various steps toward the concentration of all Americans had been carried out, and finally, on November 5th, the Imperial Edict, putting California under the protection of the Emperor of Japan and decreeing the expulsion of all "aliens" was promulgated. At the same time the treaty was concluded with most of the Mexican chieftains, acknowledging the protectorate of Japan over Lower California and the Western States of Mexico, and that of England over the Yucatan Peninsula and the Eastern States.

The execution of this savage sentence against the people of California provided one of the strangest and most terrible spectacles in history. To be sure, life and been hard under the conqueror. Besides the infinitely humiliating experience of being ruled by the yellow man, the people of California had often to endure hunger; and constantly white girls and women were disappearing, no one could learn where, but all could guess; no remonstrance, no plea, could extend the suave assurances of the Japanese rulers to a real search of the barracks and camps and the officers' quarters. Few of the girls whose stricken parents mourned their sudden disappearance ever returned.

To some there was, therefore, a welcome prospect in the expulsion order; yet it was a tragic pilgrimage that crossed the

mountains by every road, driven on by Japanese bayonet and
Cossack knout, during the last two weeks of November. All that
was Home, all that was Hope, all that was Life, was left behind,
and a little gold, never more than half or three-quarters of the value
of the property taken, was all that the conquerors gave them to start
life anew. Many a hasty grave marks the path of that weeping
pilgrimage; even more are buried just cross the borders, where the
facilities hastily gathered by the people of neighboring States to
care for and distribute were woefully inadequate, so that starvation,
thirst, disease, and despair claimed many a victim. On November
15, 1920, there were only a handful of hunted white refugees in the
mountains of California; a State was held by something like
357,000 troops, of whom 80,000 were Russians, a few Mexicans,
the rest Japanese; the Hindus had been sent back to British
Columbia, to join England's plans farther East.

EXPELLED FROM CALIFORNIA

"It was a tragic pilgrimage that crossed the mountains."

Hyphenated-Americans and Others

VIII

I am told that the effect of the news of England's declaration of war had, in New York at least, and doubtless in other cities, a strange and terrible effect. Millions of people seemed all at once to lose their grip. Businessmen closed their officers and went home in a daze, workingmen spontaneously stopped work.

Then the heroic temper rose, and great spontaneous meetings were held everywhere at which the flag was waved and the national anthems sung between patriotic speeches. The sun was setting through its haze of smoke over the river as the city found its true expression in patriotic determination. The leaders of this return to courage were chiefly, though not exclusively, citizens of Irish and German blood, affiliated with or influenced by the Irish and German organizations, and the Irish and German daily and weekly papers. Their reading of recent events, their anticipations, their abiding sentiments, had been very different from those of the people who had depended entirely on the ordinary daily press and the weekly and monthly so-called "reviews."

They had put no faith in the fair words of England, and had bitterly resented the admonitions to trust the safety and dignity of their great nation to the English Navy and the Sikh and Ghurka soldiery. So convinced that some of the Irish-American and German-American leaders had been that the very catastrophe which now had befallen was imminent, that they had been very busily recruiting the Irish Volunteers and the Turner Militia and drilling them into something like very respectable military organizations, totaling in the various cities nearly 50,000 men.

As the sun set on that wild evening of July 16th, the music of a fife and drum corps startled the thousands who still lingered in the

downtown streets of New York City, listening to orators on

wagons, on stoops, in motor-cars. The stirring strains of Yankee

Doodle set the air dancing and stilled the oratory; and up through

Cortlandt Street a column of rugged men in Khaki; in columns of

four, with rifles on shoulder, marched steadily amid ecstatic

cheers. Two men on horseback led the line, clearing a way for the

American flag. They were not regulars. They were not militia.

Behind the flag came a huge canvas "transparency" and on each

face the world "Irish" was stricken through with heavy black lines,

and the world "American" inserted before "Volunteers." The

whole sign read thus:

FIRST

AMERICAN

VOLUNTEERS.

Men of America! Enlist!

All Depends On You!

THE VERY LIFE OF LIBERTY,

THE VERY EXISTENCE OF THE REPUBLIC,

ARE AT STAKE!

FALL IN!

SHOW YOUR STUFF!

FOLLOW US AND ENLIST! ENLIST!

THE "HYPHENATED" AMERICANS

"All night men stood in line and took the oath."

Six companies passed; then, behind a brass band which blared the deep music of The Star Spangled Banner, another transparency had the words "German-American Turners" crossed through, and the words "Second American Volunteers" emblazoned. Five companies followed this.

These were the new American Minute Men. These were as many as could be quickly summoned of the Irish-American and German-American volunteer patriots of the near-by cities of Jersey. Almost simultaneously, full regiments of each organization started from a mobilization at Park Avenue and 59th Street–the Irish and Germans of New York. Up Broadway moved one column, down Broadway the other. Tens upon tens of thousands of cheering citizens fell into line; the news spread East and West, and the huge processions found ever more and greater crowds awaiting, to be caught up in the delirious fervor and swung into line in response to the deep roar of "Fall in, fall in, Enlist, enlist, enlist!" to which columns were moving in martial measure. Only as they passed the newspaper offices–the *Times* and *Herald*, uptown; the *Tribune, Sun, World,* and *Globe,* downtown–the music of the bans and fife and drum corps changed to a Dead March, and the crowds yelled imprecations at their betrayers and shook their fists at the blank-bulletin boards.

Both columns turned into Madison Square and formed their lines along the outer paths, shutting in the green. Each of the New York regiments had been accompanied by a great canvas-covered wagon, and from these were produced tents, table, chairs, writing

utensils, banners, and great piles of printed paper forms, cards and

badges. Then, with the drums throbbing and the brown lines

standing there leaning on their rifles, the thousands of citizens

whose wills were firm to volunteer, were admitted through

numerous gaps, and under erected tents they were hastily inspected

as to elementary physical fitness, and those who passed this

inspection were given pledges to sign, cards certifying their

membership, and badges in lieu of uniforms.

These pledges bound them to hold themselves at the disposal

of the commanders of the American Volunteers for military service

against the enemies of the United States, unless otherwise called

on for the service by the Government, to attend drills nightly and at

all other possible times until further orders, to purchase equipment

if their means permitted, otherwise to contribute to a fund for the

purchase of equipment, to endeavor to make such arrangements

with regard to their business or employment as would leave them

free to go to the front or to camp in case of call, or, in case of vital

need, to go to the front despite any private entanglements and at

any personal sacrifice. The cards were arranged for stamping in acknowledgement of attendance at drills.

All night men stood in line and passed into the tents and took the oath; all the next day the same, while the khaki-clad men slept and watched by turn. Before noon the next day over 12,000 men had been pledged and enrolled, and still the huge crowds of citizens pressed forward, never tiring of the martial and patriotic songs they sang, nor of the forceful speeches made to them by selected orators clad in khaki.

Perhaps the most active personality among those who made this splendid first step toward defending the threatened Republic was Congressman O'Hagan, one of the two mounted officers who led the Jersey companies to New York that night. It was largely due to his clear vision and convincing speech that so many men were ready; it was largely due to his foresight, his labors, and his success in raising funds that these companies were so well equipped for the work they suddenly set under way that night.

O'Hagan was familiar with the contents of the note from Sir Edward Grey which Sir M. de C. Findlay, the English Ambassador, had presented on April 23rd, and which had never been given to the public. From that day he began, with the co-operation of others who saw the danger as clearly as he, to prepare for the stroke which he was so thoroughly convinced would be struck. When the news of the blow-up in the Culebra Cut was received, the Irish Volunteers and the German-American Turners in every city where there was a company or regiment of either, received orders to respond to an instant call, and to report, in full uniform and equipment at any early hour every night at their headquarters; while at considerable expense a number of messengers with bicycles, motorcycles, and automobiles, and a staff of girls who could be quickly sent to public telephone stations, were restrained, in several cities, at headquarters during the 15th and 16th.

Thus was made possible the rapid mobilization which put the American Volunteers on the streets of Paterson, Jersey City, Newark, New York, Boston, Philadelphia, Chicago, Milwaukee, Butte, Montana, and other cities at the psychological moment, and the perfected equipment which made it possible to enroll 200,000 volunteers within a week.

Congressman O'Hagan stayed no longer on the night of the

16th than was necessary to see the work in full and glorious swing.
Then he took the midnight train to Washington, and ere the sun
was high in conference with the leaders of Congress. The Senate
and the House of Representatives assembled at noon on the 17th
with the situation well in the hands of the leaders.

Bluff old Champ Clark, Speaker of the House; Representative
Kitchin, the Democratic Floor Leader, and the grizzled Jim Mann,
Republican Floor Leader, in turn made brief, powerful appeals for
the quick adoption of necessary measures of defense. With genuine
emotion these men referred briefly and bitterly to the treachery of
the enemies, and the faults and blindness of the rules and
politicians of the country. There was no indecision in the attitude
they now assumed and the steps they now proposed to make up for
the past faults and to meet the present situation.

A huge war appropriation was passed, a great bond issue in
small denominations ordered, and many public works, for which
money had already been appropriated, were ordered stopped.
Provisions was made for increasing army and the militia, a small
Congressional Committee was appointed to assist the War
Department in the purchase and manufacture of equipment, and

power was vested in them to compel manufacturers to make necessary articles of military nature, and to sell such things to the Government at satisfactory prices, under threat of confiscation of plant and product at prices set by the Congressional Committee. The Constitutionality of this law was not brought into question, nor was it left possible for any legal action to half the proposed processes or call them into question till after the fact. It was felt that no court would dare question the interpretation of the Constitution as demanding primarily the conservation of the safety of the Nation; and it was well understood that the venerable Fundamental Law; which in ordinary times stand like Gibraltar, was quite used to being treated as a vital, pragmatic principle in times of crisis.

Among the other measures passed was a Volunteer law, framed by O'Hagan but introduced by Mr. Kitchin. It provided for the acceptance by the Government of services of volunteer companies, battalions, regiments, and brigades, under their selected officers, organized as nearly as possible on the lines of standard American army units, uniformed as nearly as possible in conformity with the regular fatigue uniform of the army. These volunteer organizations were to be subject to the command of the highest regular army commanders in their districts, but were to have the option of staying within their home districts, as specifically delimited in the bill, or of going out of those districts as their own officers might decide.

"A huge war appropriation was passed."

They were to be paid by the Government, a small salary per man for drill attendance, the regular army pay for active service.

Finally, it was provided, with as much deference as possible to the Constitution, that all employers whose business was in any degree inter-State, or advertised in newspapers or other publications which were carried by the United States mail, must continue to pay employees who were absent in actual military duty for certain specified periods, and in case of absence for longer periods, must continue such employees on their rolls and restore them to their positions upon their discharge from service.

By specific provision of this bill, the volunteers then encamped and in process of enrollment in New York were designated the First and Second American Volunteers, and their home territory was limited to the States of New York, New Jersey, Connecticut, and Vermont. By specific provision, Shawn O'Hagan was made commander of these two brigades, with the title of Brigadier-General. There was no bar to the organization of other volunteer units in the same territory, but O'Hagan was to command all volunteers in his district, under the regular army General in command of the Department of the East.

The Senate, meanwhile, had undertaken no legislative work, but, pending the arrival of the House Bills, had listened to forceful and bitter speeches. All parties and persuasions joined in bitter denunciations of the Pacifists. Alas, how belated was this return to reason and rationalism! The climax was reached when, after the speeches of Senators Kern, Lewis, and O'Gormann, the Democratic Leaders, and Senators Penrose and Cummings, respectively leaders of the Conservative Republicans and the Progressive Republicans, and after the thrilling denunciations of England by Senators Chamberlain, of Oregon, and Borah, of Idaho, two men who had always suspected the English purposes, John Sharp Williams, of Mississippi, and Henry Cabot Lodge, of Massachusetts, were supported into the chamber.

Both of these veterans and venerable legislators were now old and very feeble; both had risen from sick beds to attend this session. Both had been the spokesmen of Anglophilism and Pacifism; and now, in speeches which hushed the chamber, each made, in sorrow and shame, his recantation.

Then the Clerk of the House appeared, accompanied by delegations of the leaders of both parties. The House Bills were read and passed. It was a splendid demonstration of how Congress could do business when it wanted to. Immediately upon passage of the last bill, a delegation of Senators and Representatives, one hundred strong, carried the measures in person to the White House, where the President, apprised by the leaders of the nature of the bills, and fully agreeing on the urgency of the situation, at once affixed his signature to each. The ceremony was one of solemn silence.

The next day Brigadier-General Shawn O'Hagan was back in New York. The city authorities opened all the parks to the volunteers as drill-grounds, and arranged for the drilling of platoons of policemen and firemen. But the marvel of the city was the speed with which arms, ammunition, and uniforms were produced. It was revealed that the leaders who had foreseen the situation that now existed had raised sufficient funds–chiefly among Irish contractors and German brewers–to secure several thousand stands of arms and a great supply of ammunition, as well as hundreds of thousands of blank cartridges.

It was not known till later that this had been possible only by making the munitions manufacturers believe that the purchasers were agents of a South American government. Furthermore, options had been secured on the outputs of certain mills and factories making grey flannel shirts, khaki shirts, and khaki trousers. From the first days, therefore, thanks to the hyphenated-Americans, the volunteer recruits had the advantage to their *morale* of drilling in a sort of uniform, with rifles; of practicing tactics and maneuvers to the accompaniment of the martial music of blank cartridges; and of practicing target and volley firing with real ammunition in the larger parks.

Under a provision of the Volunteer Law, funds were immediately drawn from the sub-treasury for the purchase of sturdy shoes, cartridge belts and bandoliers, haversacks, canteens, puttees, caps, and more rifles and ammunition; and the generous contributions of the volunteers themselves, and of the citizens, put large sums of money at the disposal of the commanders of these forces.

Other companies and regiments were organized independently of the First and Second Volunteers, but in co-operation with them and under the energetic management of General O'Hagan and a staff of competent men. In other cities much the same development took place, but nowhere quite so energetically and successfully as the great city of New York.

New York Bombarded–Thousands Dead and Dying–Big Buildings Destroyed!

IX

At dawn on the 18th of July a British fleet presented its

compliments to Fort Hancock, on Sandy Hook, in the form of 15-

shells. Fort Hancock returned the compliment with a few 16-inch

projectiles. No damage was done on either side. The excitement in

New York did not approach a panic, because every effort was

made to re-assure the people of the adequacy of our coast defenses.

Besides, the great dreadnoughts *New York* and *Brooklyn* were in the harbor, the latter, to be sure, just out of dry-dock in the Navy Yard in her home city, and not in commission. Also, the good light cruisers *Hudson* and *Chesapeake* were in the Bay, and the two new sea-going submarines *Sampson* and *Schley*. One older submarine was in commission and three were undergoing alterations at the Navy Yard.

"A British fleet presented its compliments to Fort Hancock."

Little did the people understand how valueless a few ships, even of the best type, are when confronted by an overwhelming fleet. The function of a navy is to overwhelm the enemy on the high seas by being concentrated in superior force at every point of contact; but the American Navy was scattered, some, as we have seen in the Canal, blockaded, others in Chesapeake Bay, New York Harbor, Delaware Bay, and Boston Harbor–all blockaded!

During the 18th, 19th, and 20th the English ships did nothing but let New York and all ships attempting to enter it or leave it know that there was an effective blockade in force. To be sure, many of the ships were familiar with the situation, for had not America submitted to an English blockade of New York and other ports by the England Navy in 1914-15, sometimes beyond the three-mile limit, sometimes within it?

On the 19th the *Hudson* dashed out and drew the fire of the enemy in an attempt to give one of the older submarines a chance to strike, but the ruse was discovered and the submarine had to return with eager destroyers on her track. The *Hudson* was hit several times and returned with a list to port. Also, two torpedoes from as many pursuing destroyers, passing close astern, warned her of the danger of such small tactics.

The harbor was pretty adequately mined to a point a little beyond Sandy Hook, which was protected as far as it went, but how miserably inadequate that was appeared very soon. On the night of the 20th the residents of a prosperous neighborhood near Prospect Park, Brooklyn, were startled by a terrific explosion. Fear quickly changed to panic and hysteria as another, another, and another explosion occurred, and it was learned that giant shells were falling among the quiet homes of New York's chief residential Borough, slaughtering men, women, and children as they slept or walked the streets, as they talked in groups in saloons or light refreshment parlors, as they applauded moving pictures of the American Army and Navy.

From Forts Hancock and Hamilton the bombardment could, of course, be heard, and from the former, dim flashes from the devastating guns could be seen, and indicated that it was being carried on from a point near Rockaway Beach. For hours the bigger guns on Sandy Hook fired through the night, but aim was impossible. In the morning the fleet withdrew out of range, but from the decks of the ships arose squadrons of air-craft which soared away toward Brooklyn, where, hovering low, they noted calmly the destruction wrought, and returning, reported to their fleet. Again they flew over Brooklyn, hovering and circling for hours, dropping little balls of soot and flakes of glittering tinsel. Long since, English secret agents had made lists of the chief objects of destruction in New York, together with maps showing their distance from Rockaway, and the airmen were now confirming the naval officers' calculations as to ranges. Improved instruments made it possible to follow the heights and distances of the planes and to make notes by which the guns would be fired in the dark.

All day the frightened exodus from Brooklyn continued; at night the great guns took up their work again. First, the encampment of the volunteers at Prospect Park was made untenable. Next, a number of great industrial plants were tried for, and several of them wrecked. Then the great shells began to fall around the Borough Hall. The pretty Hall of Records was blown asunder. The Eagle Tower was toppled and the Hotel Claredon set afire. One shell wrecked the elevated railway structure above and the subway below Fulton Street, snuffing out three-score lives and closing those two ways of escape. This thing was almost beyond the nerves of the bravest to endure. Death came out of nowhere, in so cruel a form, mangling, maiming, killing the babe and mother whom the agonized father had strove to protect; giving no quarter, giving no chance, making no distinction.

Then suddenly the firing ceased. Some heard dim muffled explosion afar off. In the morning it was learned that the two powerful submarines had slipped out in the night. The *Sampson* had been unable to find a target in the dark; the *Schley* had "got" the swift battle cruiser *Inflexible*, which sank instantly with her eight 12-inch guns. Furthermore, a huge battleship of the *Overpowering* type had been hit by a mortar shell from Fort Hancock, and had hastily retired the swarm of destroyers which attempted to run them down.

This sharp stroke by the defending forces put new heart enough into the people of New York to stay the panic which visitation of murderous shells had bred. By the same token, it made singularly inept the announcements which formed the chief items in the newspapers on the morning of the 22nd, that a great meeting to urge the Government to ask an armistice and to propose to the

Nation's enemies that all matters between them to be submitted to arbitration, would be held the next day in Carnegie Hall, which overflow meetings in Central Park. The principal speakers would be Charles W. Eliot, Nicholas Murray Butler, John Hays Hammond, James Brown Scott, David Starr Jordan, Newell Dwight Hillis, and John Wesley Hill. It was not revealed that William J. Bryan, William H. Taft, Alton B. Parker, and Jane Addams had indignantly refused to continue their peace propaganda at this crisis.

The newspapers urged the support of all rational people for this movement, in special attacks emblazoned on the front pages. The news of the America success during the night was printed with little acclaim on an inner page, but it had already been spread throughout the city, and as the infantry of this new attempt at betrayal dawned on the crowds of people gathered to cheer the victory, it needed but a few fiery speeches to set mobs of infuriated men racing for the newspaper buildings.

The *Herald,* still the organ of French finance; the *Times,* still the possessor of 250,000 shares of English Mariconi stock; the *Sun*, still edited by unnaturalized Englishmen and mortgaged to

English money-lenders; the *World,* still closely allied with the English press bureau; the *Press*, still heavily interested in U.S. Steel and Bethlehem Steel, which had continued for six years to make huge profits selling the materials of war to England, Japan, France, and Russia, were now vainly trying to resist the command of the Congressional Munitions Committee to make munitions for the American Army–all these felt the wrath of the mob. The *Herald, Sun,* and *Press* buildings were fired; in the other plants complete wreck was made of all machinery. The city had been under martial law since the morning of the 21st, but there were few regulars there excepting drill squads engaged in teaching recruits. To the militia had been entrusted most of the work of patrolling the city, and hundreds of these joined the mobs. The plant of the Hearst papers was not touched, for the *Morning American* had famously denounced the "proposal of cowardly surrender made by traitors."

O'Hagan communicated with General Wood, who was on Governor's Island busy with administrative work, and received his permission to guard the wrecked plants, to prohibit their owners and managers from issuing their papers or any substitutes therefor from any other plants, to run the *Globe, Mail,* and *Post* as official organs, and to arrest and confine any who could be found of the men who purposed speaking at the "Arbitration" meeting the next day. Needless to say, the meeting was not held.

The blows struck in the night did not discourage the English. At noon on the 22nd their hydro-aeroplanes rose in graceful flocks and sailed over the Upper Bay and high above Manhattan. Five military planes rose from Governor's Island, together with six non-military machines, the private owners of which had just sworn in and uniformed as members of the regular army. Straight for the scattered English machines they went, and the latter collected over Brooklyn and fled like startled birds back to their fleets. One American and one English plane were brought down by guns of an English cruiser to which they approached fatally close in their battle-fury.

The whole English fleet now moved closer and began the heaviest naval bombardment history had yet known. The great guns of the huge new *Overpowering, Overwhelming,* and *Overbearing,* the great *Queen Elizabeth,* the mighty *Iron Duke,* the *King Edward VII,* the *King George V,* the *Malaya,* the *Monarch,* the *Prince George,* the *Prince of Wales*, and several lesser craft united in attack on Fort Hancock, and then, as the long line swung swiftly around, aimed in turn at Fort Wadsworth, Fort Hamilton, the battleship *New York,* which lay behind Fort Hamilton, and finally at their most distant mark, which their air-fleet was again indicating to them, the Brooklyn Naval Yard.

The roar of their guns, the answering roar from the three forts and from the *New York*, seemed to rock the towering city. The fleet was taking its chances, but its swift movement, combined with frequent twists and turns by each individual craft, made difficult targets for the forts. The American air-craft were aloft again, chiefly for the assistance of the *New York*, which, cruising about in swift zigzags behind Fort Hamilton, was equally unseen and unseeing. The rival air-squadrons left each other severely alone.

First blood was drawn by the fleet, as an incalculable weight of metal from 15-inch and 13-inch guns crumpled a section of the defense at Fort Hancock and put a 12-inch mortar out of action. Soon afterward a distance hit was scored by Fort Wadsworth, one of the smaller, older cruisers being damaged above decks. Then a mortar shell from Hancock tore away a portion of the bow of the

Queen Elizabeth, and a 16-inch shot damaged one of the forward guns of the *Malaya*.

Meanwhile, the first shot from the *Overpowering* had struck near the Navy Yard, and within a few moments nine shells from the *Overbearing* and *Overwhelming* had landed in the Yard. One of them tore two of the submarines to pieces, another put the forward turret of the *Brooklyn* out of all usefulness, a third one took one of that ship's funnels away. Returning from the position near the shore from which these hits had been made–across the whole of Brooklyn–the *Overbearing* was caught by shells from Hamilton and Wadsworth which, however, only wrecked a few of her smaller guns and caused some casualties. Despite the favorable range, the Hancock's guns failed to score at this turn. The full power of the greatest guns of the fleet, now turned on Hancock, and failed to breach a wall or find a concealed gun. The shots of the *New York* constantly fell short, but she herself was not hit throughout the action.

Again the head of the English line approached close to Rockaway Beach. Again the united might of the main batteries of the three leading ships, this time joined by the *Iron Duke, King*

Edward VII, King George V, Monarch, Prince George, and *Prince of Wales,* was directed at the unseen target, the Navy Yard, thirteen miles distant. Across the whole of Brooklyn the great shells whistled shrilly, and fell within the Yard like a bombardment of meteors. For more than ten minutes they came. At the end of that time, when they stopped on signal of their air-scouts, the Brooklyn Navy Yard was a scene of ruin indescribable.

The great warship named for the Borough was shattered by explosions caused by shells that reached her boilers and magazines. *The Hudson,* also at the Yard for repairs after her dash on the 19th, was sunk at the dock. Most of the machine shops were wrecked, the arsenal was blown out of existence and several naval guns lying about unmounted were shattered. The barracks were aflame. Hundreds of marines, blue-jackets, and workmen lay dead, or moaning with agony of mangled wounds.

While these dreadful volleys were delivered, the guns of Wadsworth, Hamilton, and Hancock, obedient to orders from headquarters, suddenly concentrated on the swarm of torpedo boat destroyers which sped ceaselessly to and fro between the great ships and the mine-fields. Shells rained about the little craft and on them. Two were sunk and several damaged in the five minutes before the fire suddenly ceased. But as they scattered before this sudden punishment, the guardians of England's dreadnoughts did not fail to apprehend its purpose, and keen eyes soon detected the periscopes of three American submarines. Three-score light rapid-firing guns were turned upon then. The *Sampson* was fatting struck, but as she sank she torpedoed one of the grey scorpions that stung her to death. The *Schley* submerged and escaped; the third submarine, one of the older craft, defective in design when launched, and unimproved by years of tinkering, failed to work at the critical moment–and would not submerge–and the next moment was submerged forever by a dozen bits.

Once more the ships circled, throwing streams of shells at the forts, most of them now hitting, but having little effect for all their power. Had the guns of the forts been adequately manned, the game would have been decidedly bad for the fleet, but now in the sudden hour of trial the effect of the permanent shortage of coast defense troops was seen in slow action. A couple of funnels knocked awry were the only hits scored by the defenders on this turn, and once more the English ships drew close to Rockway.

Aided by their air-scouts, now high up and far away, but easily observed through glasses, the English Navy presented its final testimonial to that Anglo-Saxon community of interest which had so long fascinated America. This time the target was Manhattan itself. High over Brooklyn the shells whistled, scores of them, 1,500, 1,800 pounds, a ton in weight, diabolical in power!

The unique and wonderful architectural achievement, Lower New York, with its pinnacles actually neighboring the clouds, its enormous buildings harboring the brain-cells and nerve-centers of all the business which billions of American wealth sustains, suddenly felt the shock of those irresistible messengers of treachery and destruction. Steel ribs were wracked and proud crests tumbled.

One shot struck the Woolworth Building just at the base of the tower. That incredibly delicate white fabric shivered from its deep dug base to its gilded peak up in the hushed air; then a terrifying sound, as if a huge live thing were shrieking, accompanied the slow toppling of the tower, as the few steel girders not shattered by the explosion bent beneath the weight–bent, snapt! Down it plunged, dropping great white stones, dropping airy Gothic ornaments, dropping little shrieking human beings; till it crashed

the Post Office Building and lay across Broadway and Park Row.

THE BOMBARDMENT OF NEW YORK

"One shot struck the Woolworth Building."

Another shell tore a huge hole through the Equitable Building; the City Investing tower was clipped off at the 24th floor; the Park Row Building horribly shattered; the beautiful little City Hall crushed like a paper box; the huge Municipal Building reduced to a horrible tangle of ruins, crushing the lives out of thousands of trapped men and women. The Brooklyn and Manhattan Bridges escaped, with the exception of a fragmentary clipping of one tower of the former. To be sure, this so terrified the thousands of refugees, who, fleeing from Brooklyn, dared not enter New York, that scores of them leapt from the structures and perished miserably in the waters. But that was only an incident in a terrible day.

After five minutes the firing suddenly ceased. The mortars and 16-inch guns of the forts had at last made hits whose hints could not be ignored by the enemy. The great *Malaya*, of 27,500 tons, launched in 1915, mounting eight 15-inch guns, was pierced by several shells which found her boilers and magazines, and in a series of dreadful explosions she shook to pieces and sank a tangled wreck. The *Overwhelming* and *Prince of Wales* were severely struck, also, and shells came too close for comfort to the

King George V and the *Monarch.* Admiral Jellicoe decided that that phase of the game was up, and withdrew his whole fleet out of range as the sun went low in the West.

The dreadful bombardment and their ghastly effects were in complete accord with the teaching of that pet of the American Press, Lord Fisher, whose prescription for England was the instant and ruthless destruction of as many of the enemy as possible, with especial attention to women and children. It was, however, in accord with the laws of war; New York was a fortified town, subject to bombardment. Its forts were almost adequate to defend it, but the American navy should have made that defense complete. And the American navy had been scattered, as it had been weakened, by the men who taught the American people that the Navy of England would protect them!

It only needs to be said here that after this the English fleet confined itself to blockading (a few cruisers closing Long Island Sound) with occasional long-range bombarding of Fort Hancock, until that night, a few weeks later, when the *Schley* slipped out and torpedoed the *Iron Duke.* After that Admiral Jellicoe conducted his blockade on the typical English plan, on the open sea, hundreds of mile from port. His light cruisers and destroyers, nevertheless, kept watch along the Jersey and Delaware Coasts, far from New York, but sufficient to intercept any coastwise traffic. The *Schley*, in a subsequent attack on one of this flotilla, got its ship, but was itself hit by a torpedo from a destroyer, and sank with all on board.

On the evening of the 22nd of July and all that night, New York was a city of horror and fear. Less than a week ago it had seemed immune from the harsh chances of war as at any time during the hundred years since the Treaty of Ghent. Compared with the cities of Europe its lot was charmed. Now its proudest towers were mere disfiguring heaps of brick and scrap iron, thousands of its citizens and defenders were dead or wounded, hundreds of thousands fought for ways to flight, northward into Westchester and Connecticut, westward across the Hudson. Fleeing, they suffered all the hardships of hunger, homelessness, separation from kin and friends.

Fortunately, the mere pressure of the numbers attempting to leave, with the resulting congestion and accidents, tended to check the movement, and the next morning the news of the punishment meted out to the enemy, coupled with official proclamations positively assuring the people that the forts had now mastered the ranges sufficiently to prevent any further attempt by the fleet to maintain a position from which it could shell the city, largely revived the people's courage.

It had occurred to certain of the commanders of the defense and their advisers that the English fleet would hardly have shelled Lower New York, where customarily so vast a sum in securities owned by Englishmen were stored, and where the offices of so many corporations largely controlled by English money, had not something occurred which changed this condition in some degree or other? The investigations now set on foot disclosed that an astonishing liquidation and conversion of securities, an astonishing withdrawal of capital, had quietly taken place, first over a long period of time, then suddenly in the last few days; and that not only had much gold left the country for Canada, during the preceding weeks, but that under cover of the excitement since the 16th, vast sums from the Gorgan banks and certain others had been shipped north, actually passing through the enemy lines into Canada and through the blockading lines to England.

J. P. Gorgan himself and a number of other financiers and

bankers had disappeared; later to turn up where they really belonged, in England. It was later learned also that the English Government had made provisions for the reimbursement of Englishmen who might lose on American securities and other property due to the war, out of Government funds which were planned to be supplied by the indemnities levied on American communities; but furthermore, it was planned to secure the safety of much or all of this English capital by threat of confiscation of great amounts of American capital which had recently been invested in English securities by the Gorgan and other banks acting as agents for confiding American capitalists and investors.

England and Her Whelps

X

Between 1915 and 1920 the Dominion of Canada had

increased its standing and reserve forces from 80,000 to 140,000.

American newspapers failed to report this and suppressed the

warnings which watchful men uttered. By July 16, 1920, public

and secret mobilizations had put about 100,000 of these Canadian

troops on a war footing, mostly concentrated near Montreal. There

were also 5,000 English troops at Montreal, and 15,000 at Halifax.

The latest arrivals of Hindus at Vancouver brought the number of those dark warriors to 60,000, of whom 20,000 (I give round numbers) were sent with the Japanese through Washington and Oregon to California, about 10,000 were encamped near Winnipeg, and about 30,000 went East, the last of them reached Hamilton, Ontario, on July 26th.

On July 20th Russia and France declared war on the United States. The reasons given were the "anarchy created on the American Continents by the tyrannical pretentions and acts of the United States Government and the necessity of protecting" Russian and French interests in the Western Hemisphere and on the oceans. The actual facts were that Russia was hopelessly dependent on France and England for money, that Russia and France were bound by secret treaties to assist England, and that the English diplomats were able to offer certain luscious bribes.

Since the Peace of Brussels, England had continued to hold Calais. The French nation was too feeble to protest vigorously, the French politicians were England's property, Germany looked on with amusement, letting the English know that the slightest move towards strengthening the somewhat battered and antiquated defenses would cause Germany to strike instantly; but England held on in hope of achieving its purpose by underhanded means. That hope showed itself more and more illusory, and by the Spring of 1920 England was ready to make the restoration of Calais, one of the items of the price offered the French. It was further promised that France would receive New Orleans and the State of Louisiana. An excellent case for the Justice of the restoration of this territory to France was made out by French and English apologists–quite as good a case as the French claim to Alsace-Lorraine.

It was also hinted, not promised, that parts of the Province of Quebec south of St. Lawrence, together with the States of Maine, New Hampshire, and Northern New York might be given to France. All reference to the manner of English acquisition of the formerly French Canada was discreetly avoided, even as, in 1914-15, the trivial and unreal French grievance against Germany entirely hid the long, bitter record of English invasion, bullying, and intriguing against France.

As to Russia, the results of the Great War had forced her again to the Far East. Her hope of possessing Constantinople and Danzig, if not Hamburg and Bremen, was crushed. All her huge uncouth power was directed again toward the Pacific. The relations

between Russia and Japan were becoming strained, and the English

diplomats had indeed tried to precipitate a conflict; but neither

Russia nor Japan dared. Perhaps after this war on America, the

English statesmen thought, Russia would be strong enough and

Japan weakened enough for the attack to be made. So Russia was

offered the division of Alaska between her and Canada and a new

large loan. The loan was to be spent in improving the Trans-

Siberian Railway and in building a fleet of Russian merchant

steamers on the Pacific. Russian warships were to be built, also,

but that was hidden, or conspirators thought it was hidden, from

Japan. Nikolai Nikolaivitch, Sazonoff, and Goremykin and their

pals would form a contracting company to improve the railways;

they would form a steamship company to receive the Government

subsidy for building ships, and they would have the ships built by a

construction company who would also be themselves. So they

were ready to consider this bribe, for there were always millions of

moujiks and Cossacks to command; millions who knew naught but

to obey, even to death, even under military leaders with the record

of Nikolai Nikolaivitch.

The Canadians Are Victorious

"Canadian troops seized all bridges across the Niagara River."

By July 26th a French army corps had completed

disembarkation at Montreal–the first company having arrived on

July 20th, showing that they had started before the French

declaration of war, even as early as in July, 1914, thousands of

French Colonials, that is, black Africans, had been brought to

Marseilles long before Germany had either mobilized or demanded

that France refrain from mobilizing. Sikhs and Ghurkas meanwhile

continued to arrive at Vancouver.

During the night of July 16th and 17th Canadian troops

seized all bridges across the Niagara River, near the Falls, and that

between Bridgeburg, Ont., and Black Rock, N.Y., seven miles

from Buffalo. In the morning they were excellently entrenched,

and over their trenches gleamed rifle-barrels and machine guns.

The militia of Buffalo and Northern Tonawanda were

mobilized on the 17th, strenuous efforts were made to muster the

companies to something like full strength, and on the evening of

the 18th they joined forces and attacked the trenches at Black Rock.

They mustered about 3,000 men, including a battery of light

artillery. Halting on the edge of the zone of fire they entrenched,

and during the night placed their artillery. With the coming of

dawn they opened fire.

After an hour of shelling, which had a visible effect on one

section of the enemy's line, the Colonel commanding ordered an

advance. It was undertaken with great skill and steadiness, but

when it came under full fire of machine guns in the open it broke down, and nearly 300 men were missing from the broken ranks that re-formed before the American artillery. The shelling of the Canadian trenches begun again, but ere long the ammunition was exhausted. Then the Canadians charged, in superior force, and the militiamen, disheartened by their inability to sustain a military action through lack of means wherewith to fight, made the best of a hasty retreat to Buffalo, leaving their useless field guns to the invader. The bridgeheads continued to be held by well-entrenched Canadians.

During the night of the 16th-17th an invasion in greater force and apparently of much more ominous character had developed on the Eastern border of the State. Moving with a speed and a perfection of plan which told of long preparation, trains full of Canadians and English rolled into New York and Vermont on both sides of Lake Champlain. Long before dawn Plattsburgh and Burlington were in their possession; before noon of the 17th their advance halted at Ticonderoga and Montcalm Landing, and they were in complete possession of the New York side and greater part of the Vermont shore.

The ruins of Fort Ticonderoga were visited by a party of

Canadian and English officers. It was here, in the early days of the Revolution, that Ethan Allen, commanding a party of "Green Mountain Boys" had surprised the British garrison and forced them to surrender "in the name of the great Jehovah and the Continental Congress!" On this latter occasion a Canadian captain named Allen–one of the Allens of Montreal–climbing to a high point of the ancient fort, exclaimed "in the name of King George and the great Jehovah we here undo the work of the Continental Congress!"

On the evening of the 17th two passenger steamers on Lake George were captured at Baldwin, the northernmost landing on that most beautiful and historic of American lakes. On the 18th two yachts of considerable size and great speed, the property of wealthy Canadians who had purchased them the year before, issued from their boat houses near the upper end of Lake Champlain, neatly armored with this steel plates and bristling with light cannon and machine guns. These gun-boats proceeded to round up everything they found afloat in or out of harbor, convoying all desirable prizes to Plattsburgh. For two weeks troops continued to move down Champlain and George along shore and by boat. The garrisons at Lake George and at Whitehall, just south

of Lake Champlain, remained for some time the southernmost

points of the invasion.

The Capture of Fort Ticonderoga

"We here undo the work of the Continental Congress!"

For some fortunate reason no surprise attack was made on the

army post of Burlington the night the city was entered. The

commander of the troops there, entirely ignorant of the strength of the enemy, did not attempt street fighting in the dark, and after dawn the invaders were in sufficient force to hold the town to its outer edges, and the American artillery could not be used without sacrificing American non-combatants. The invaders made an attack in force, and at the same time the two armed yachts shelled a flank of the American forces. Retreat became inevitable, and was affected in good order, but the total of American losses in killed, wounded, and captured amounted to nearly a battalion. The remainder made their way, on receipt of orders, to Watervliet, the site of one of the chief government arsenals, near Troy.

Meanwhile, along the Niagara River, all was as quiet as in the pipingest time of peace. The Canadians merely held their positions on the American side. Very efficient cavalry patrols on the Canadian side prevented any information coming through with the exception of occasional "American refugees," as they described themselves, who made reports, which, of course, were telegrammed to New York and Washington, that the whole province of Ontario was practically without troops beyond the few companies along the Niagara. On the other hand, men who made their way through either the Adirondacks or the Green Mountains to Albany reported that the forces continually moving down the Lake Champlain were countless hosts.

One of the curious and dangerous results of America's long deference to English teachings soon appeared in the weird military plans which were urged for the defense of the New York. With an army accumulating its forces 190 miles to the North, and enemy forces holding the bridges into the State from Ontario on the Northwest, it was seriously urged that part of the little defending army should be deployed across Long Island and stationed at points in Connecticut and New Jersey.

Grave authorities on military matters and cheap fabricators of sensational fiction had for years been calling attention to Germany as a probable foe. Germany would land her troops somewhere on the coast, and, overwhelming our defensive forces, capture our cities and our coast defenses. It was a fixed idea in many minds, therefore, that an enemy was going to land somewhere on the coast. It had never been hinted by authorities, fiction-makers, or newspapers that England might be our foe–England, with Canada all prepared as a superb base from which to strike; and now, with

England striking through Canada, it was impossible to make some people see the real state of affairs. Some, perhaps, did not want to see.

Clearer minds saw that with Canada as a base England would not, unless the Canadian invasion failed, attempt a landing on the coasts of Connecticut or New Jersey or Long Island. The Hudson was not, for its whole length, an easy road for invasion if serious opposition were offered, but if availed of quickly before opposition could be organized, by that force which did not have to be transported, but was already mobilized at our gates, the army of Canada, it was a superb line of advance. It was the road, also, for the forces sent from the Pacific.

England, if the blows were struck quickly, need send no more than a few thousand Tommies as a mere formality; her ships could stay in their merchant traffic, her men be kept at work in the factories profiting by the boom in trade and manufacture which is England's first and most immediate profit from a war. It was clear enough that there was no present danger on the coast.

The New York militia had been brought, by the great work of Major-General O'Ryan, to its full strength, that is to say, it was a complete division, something over twenty thousand men of arms.

About 5,000 were in the Western part of the State. The militia of

the Fifth Division, comprising the New England States, was

available to the extent of about 10,000 men; it could not be

mobilized to full strength and the Governor of Massachusetts

refused to allow and but a small portion of the forces of that State

to leave the vicinity of Boston.

Counting the men in retreat from Burlington to Watervliet,

those of Governor's Island and others in the New England and

Central Atlantic States, there should have been about 22,500

regulars available to the defense of New York. Add to these 25,000

militia and perhaps 60,000 volunteers really available east of

Syracuse–the numbers enrolled was much larger–but of very

varying degrees of usefulness, and the force was none too large for

resistance in one direction alone.

Nevertheless, nearly 10,000 regulars were promptly ordered to

defend Washington, and the militia and volunteers of all States

near the District of Columbia were also concentrated there.

Absolutely no danger threatened the Capital. To be sure, a

considerable fraction of a fleet was blockaded in the

Chesapeake–the *Utah, Alabama, Colorado*, and some older ships, for new submarines–only one at this time in commission–some odds and ends of old submarines, and a flotilla of destroyers. The blockading fleet consisted of the new English battle cruisers *Leopard, Unicorn, Intrepid, Invulnerable, Insuperable, Imperturbable,* and several other powerful ships, with a flotilla of destroyers and clouds of aeroplanes. They American fleet could not get out, the English could not get in, for the forts were formidable and the waters mined. A movement against Washington by land would have been a bit of sentimental folly beyond the English, so long as they had practical business like capturing New York to do. Nevertheless troops were called there.

Before the first action in defense of New York was begun, about 3,000 men had been enlisted in the regular force at New York–half as many as applied, all that could be handled. Say, then, there were about 100,000 men of all sorts available for this defense of New York. Twenty thousand were promptly distributed at what were fancied to be good strategic points along the coast. This action was taken on command from Washington. Major-General Wood at once entered a strong protest.

While action on his protest was pending the "Day of Assassinations" occurred. England had sent as Ambassador to the United States Sir M. de C. Findlay. His chief fame was that, as English Minister to Norway, he had planned the attempted assassination of Sir Roger Casement, Irish Nationalist envoy to Germany. This, with the attempts on Enver Pasha, Talaat Bey, and King Constantine, were the only failures in that program of assassination carried out by the Allies in 1914, which disposed of Jaures, Delarey, King Carlos, San Giuliano, and Witte. Subsequent investigations have revealed how Ambassador Findlay plotted the murder of Generals Wood, Barry, Funston, and O'Ryan, as well as a number of leaders of anti-English opinion. But for some reason or other instead of murdering General Wood, he was kidnapped and mysteriously imprisoned.

Before this General Wood had begun the concentration of forces along a defensive line just about Troy and Watervliet, and in a southwesterly line to the north and west of Albany. He had also set under way the preparation of a strong defense at West Point. The first position contemplated a defense against a force advancing down the line of the Erie Canal from Western New York, as well as against an advance from the Champlain region. It was farther north than General Wood thought best, but Watervliet had to be protected.

The capture of General Wood had disastrous results. Funston was needed in the West, Barry in the South was already striving to check the Japanese-Mexican invasion, Crozier was at San Francisco. The command in the East devolved on General Jones–and on General Theodore Roosevelt.

Theodore Roosevelt had, of course, begun the enlistment of a cavalry brigade as soon as the Japanese ultimatum was made public. After four years of neglect and obscurity, unable longer by any trick to catch the public eye or ear, he jumped into the limelight again with a clicking of teeth and a toss of his hat. Once more he would be Terrible Teddy; and powerful interests were not slow to equip his new Rough Riders. After the passage of the Volunteer Law his regiment had quickly expanded to a brigade and had enrolled under the Law, which he was commissioned a General of the Regular Army, and thus ranked above O'Ryan and O'Hagan.

One of the last acts of General Wood was to tell his

former associate in arms that his advocacy of armed preparedness had done more to repulse people than all of the Pacifists, that he was as responsible as any man living or dead for that blindness to the character of England which had been our undoing, and that the present war would not be a Roosevelt war if he could help it. But General Jones was quickly under the sway of that masterful, energetic personality, and that the changes in plan now made were dictated by Roosevelt.

The placing of 20,000 men along the coasts was acquiesced in, for Roosevelt asserted that Germany would undoubtedly join England very shortly out of motives of revenge upon us. His real idea seems to have been a megalomaniac conviction that the German Emperor would join England out of a desire to be revenged on him, Theodore Roosevelt. He announced that, since an invasion along the coast would certainly be made, the demonstration in the North was merely a ruse. The forces there were not sufficient to move against New York City under present conditions, but it was the intention to use them against our rear when the overseas invaders were engaging us on the coast.

"Therefore," said Teddy, showing his teeth, "*I* purpose

crushing these forces in the North by a swift blow. That is *My* plan." That became General Jones' plan, and the American lines were moved northward to the bend in the Hudson near Hudson Falls. The forces concentrated there included about 13,500 regulars, 17,000 militia, and 35,000 volunteers. Fifteen thousand volunteers were left to "garrison the city of New York." They were the Irish regiments, German regiments, an Italian regiment, a Jewish regiment, and the College Men's regiment.

General O'Hagan had encouraged and incited the formation of regiments on racial lines, as an aid to morale in the first place, in recognition of natural pride of blood, as a rebuke to Toryism, and, as he said, "to make the Hyphen forever respectable." Those who had assisted him in this fell equally with him under the displeasure of Roosevelt and Jones, including the young Harvard man of Mayflower lineage, Col. Tudor Standish, who had raised the College Men's regiment. These men whom it was intended to humiliate in this way were the best of volunteer in equipment and morale, but they bore their humiliation patiently and drilled and recruited against the day when they would be called on to retrieve the disaster that awaited Roosevelt.

What the enemy was doing was a puzzle to all who were not of Roosevelt's mind. It was obvious that a continuation of the advance begun on the night of the 16th would have enabled them to enter New York City within a few days. There would have been nothing to oppose them. They would have taken by default the huge city and the immensely valuable district around it. The possession of New York would have paralyzed resistance and afforded the quickest and easiest roads to the various prizes included in what Hudson Maxim has called the Heart of America.

They would have taken the Watervliet works and the stores of powder and the stores of powder at Iona Island on the way. In Brooklyn they would have taken the Bliss Torpedo works. They would have captured the arsenal at Governor's Island. A trip through New Jersey would have put in their possession most of the powder factories and most of the stored powder and explosives on which the American forces must depend. A little extension of this raid would have captured the Frankfort Arsenal, the Cramp Ship Yards, and the coal fields of Pennsylvania. Another expedition, a little aside from the line of the Hudson, would capture the Remington and Savage works at Ilion and Utica, and a comprehensive invasion of New England would round up practically all the remaining arms, ammunition, torpedo, torpedo boat, submarine, and ship building plants in the country.

The other wealth of this district is, of course, enormous also. New York City itself is the second greatest port and the greatest manufacturing city in the world, as well as the second greatest business center. All this was ready for the invader to take. Yet he dallied about Lake Champlain and Lake George.

As O'Hagan put it, "Was General Sam Hughes a rare damn fool, or was he calculating on our commanders being very mellow idiots? Was he spoiling Kitchener's plans, or was he carrying them out to some shrewd end?"

And the only end that could be served by delay, it seemed, was the trapping of the American forces. Canadian accounts have since disclosed that by the end of July there was something like 100,000 Canadians, 15,000 English, and 20,000 French along the line from Montreal to the lower end of Lakes Champlain and George. But there were also 30,000 Hindus, 10,000 Japanese, and 20,000 Canadians assembled at Hamilton, Ontario, and beyond that city toward Niagara.

On the 4th of August the American lines were established. 65,500 strong, behind the Hudson from Hudson Falls to west of Glen Falls. The next day a scouting party advanced to the neighborhood of the "Blood Pond" of French and Indian War days, in a narrow pass three or four miles below Lake George, an came in touch with the enemy.

That same day English spies cut the telegraph and telephone lines from Western New York in a hundred isolated places. That night trains and automobiles began to roll across the bridges over the Niagara–every car armored, many of them mounting guns and machine-guns. The next morning the citizens of Rochester were the faces of foreign soldiery; not white men, but yellow and brown men. Citizens fired, in a number of places in and around Rochester, on soldiers who had detrained to guard the tracks and to take possession of engines, cars, and stores in the railroad yards; thereafter every train that went through poured a steady fusillade from rifles and machine-guns on both sides, and occasionally a light shell was tossed playfully at a prominent steeple, a public building, or a big factor. Late in the afternoon as the last trains went through, under the urgence of strong winds these got such a start that the efforts of the fire department and the citizens was unavailing. The great city of 300,000, with its many manufactures and lovely homes, was destroyed.

The New York Central trains at this time had been equipped with wireless instruments, and train movements were controlled by wireless from the various division headquarters. The enemy had not neglected to destroy the wireless plants as they went along, but the operator on one of the trains which they intercepted at last flashed the news East and West. The first result was just beyond Syracuse that afternoon the invaders found several trains wrecked across the tracks, and the tracks torn up for a great distance. The troops were in excellent condition for marching, however, and at once set out along the line of the Erie Canal and the tracks of the West Shore and New York Central. Several companies were rushed ahead over a trolley line, and reached Canastota before dark. They were fired on during the night, and in the morning started fires in several streets away from the transportation line; then, being joined by other companies rolling in on the trolley lines, they pushed forward.

The West Shore tracks had been found intact a few miles

beyond the first break, and two or three trains were captured, armed with machine-guns, and a regiment was rushed forward on the morning of the 6th, which reached another break in the tracks on the edge of Utica about the time that the companies going forward by trolley had arrived. Several hundred citizens had armed themselves from the Remington factory and awaited the invaders behind barricades. An engagement of great intensity took place, and the Hindus and Japs paid heavily for an attempt to clear the barricades by a direct charge; but finally were able to bring machine-guns to bear in an enfilading fire, and the defenders melted away. Utica was not put to the torch because of the munitions works.

The main invading forces meanwhile were advancing by motorcar, afoot, and on horse over the longer road of the Canal. By evening of the 6th both the New York Central and West Shore tracks had been repaired, and the rear guard, who had passed through Syracuse during the night before, and consisted of a division of Canadians, took up the advance by rail. On the morning of the 7th they entered both Rome and Utica, and with the regiments in motor-cars, became the advance guard.

This method of advance was, of course, so rapid and so precarious that it could neither have been attempted nor carried out against a land armed and prepared, or against an adequate enemy in the field. But here, on this long path across the breadth of the State of New York, through a district unsurpassed in the country in populousness and wealth, the invaders had nothing to do, nothing to think of, but to advance at the greatest speed possible. There was no one to stop, no one to hinder. Companies could be thrown thirty miles in advance, divergent roads could be taken, apparent chaos could rule, communication could be abandoned, everything done so long as a rapid advance was maintained. Wireless apparatus kept every part and division in full touch with the headquarters-train of General Saito, the Japanese Commander of the army. Where unorganized opposition developed, rifle, machine-gun, field-gun, and torch were quickly available.

New York was infinitely more defenseless a prey in 1920 than it was in 1812, when an advance across the State would have been almost impossible, and when it was possible to improvise navies on Erie and Champlain and prevent the enemy's plans for invasion from ever taking shape.

From Utica on the invaders protected their lines and garrisoned all important towns. With the garrisons came looting, indemnities, and raids on near-by cities. By the evening of August 9th the advanced columns of armored trains and armored motor-cars were well out of Amsterdam on the way to Schenectady.

When news of this movement reached Generals Jones and Roosevelt, late on the afternoon of the 6th, their forces were under shrapnel-fire along their whole front, and cavalry and air-scouts reported columns of enemy steadily advancing. At dawn on the 7th the major part of the American forces crossed the Hudson and advanced in a determined effort to crush the enemy, whose full strength was yet undiscoverable. This action was conducted with the greatest tactical skill, but the folly of employing such an army in such a way was soon apparent. Lacking field-guns, none too well supplied with ammunition, utterly deficient in ammunition-trains, commissariat, hospital-trains, skilled communication troops, and aeroplanes, the various units, equally undisciplined but equally unused to fire, soon lost morale, and could have been routed by a determined onset.

But it was not the purpose of the enemy to rout them at this

time. During the evening and night the bulk of the American forces
were withdrawn across the Hudson. The next morning it was
reported that enemy cavalry had crossed the river below Fort
Edward, and that heavy columns were moving down the
Champlain Canal. A reformation of the American forces was
ordered, but an attack by the enemy along the Glen Falls-Hudson
Falls line developed in sufficient vigor to prevent this. Rumor
spread among the men that the enemy was in the rear, and
spontaneous retreats began all along the line, carrying the Generals
along with them. Some companies boarded trains, trolley cars, and
automobiles and fled as far as Saratoga Springs that day. A
battalion of volunteers was cut off Snook Creek, above
Gansevoort, and captured.

On the morning of the 9th General Roosevelt put himself at the
head of the 4,000 odd cavalry of the army and attacked a mixed
column of the enemy near Gansevoort. The engagement hung in
the balance after an hour of skirmishing, and the enemy's shrapnel
had to be avoided by either retiring or advancing. Working around
to a position that covered a good road, with level fields on both
sides, Roosevelt ordered a charge. With a shout the great line

rushed forward at the gallop, Teddy at the head, courageous, magnetic, magnificent. The enemy was dispersed and their flanking movement broken; but on the field, among the six hundred killed and wounded, lay Teddy, dead.

This courageous and sacrificial charge gave an opportunity for the head of the column to make great progress in retreat that day, under the skilled direction of General O'Ryan. They crossed the river at Schuylerville and made their way down, the next day, nearly to Mechanicsville. But the main forces, closely pressed by the enemy, were, by the morning of the 10th, a frightened mob massed between Saratoga, Ballstin, and Pound Lakes, shaken by defeat weariness, hunger, and the spectacle of their wounded suffering for lack of hospital service. And the Japanese and Hindus were in force at Schenectady. One hundred and seventy thousand men surrounded the American army.

The story of the 11th and 12th of August is familiar to my readers through the descriptions, accurate enough, cabled through England at the time; the hopeless efforts of General Jones to form a battle line, the brave but unavailing flank attack by O'Ryan along the Anthony Kill, the fury with which the disorganized units attacked the yellow and brown men when they first came in touch with them, and the final bloody Sedan.

The story of the capture of Albany, and the wanton destruction of the great New York State Capitol by rival artillerymen of Hindu, Jap, and Canadian batteries, striving to win bets placed on their skill by their officers, is also known. Fortunately, the officers in command of the Watervliet arsenal had taken it upon themselves to load all they could of guns and ammunition on trains for New York City when they heard of the advance from the West.

The next installment will picture the end of the great war of 1920.

Hyphenated-Americans Turn the Tide

XI

It does not lie within the scope of this brief history to follow in

detail the campaigns by which the great American Republic,

seemingly prostrate under the heels of the victorious Allied

invaders, was freed. Colonel Tudor Standish, the young Harvard

graduate of Mayflower descent, who raised the College Men's

Regiment, has written an exclusive history of the war, and General

Schulz, the leader of the German-American Volunteers, has

detailed the campaign in the East. Moreover, the press has made these events familiar, especially the wonderful campaign by which the military genius of General O'Hagan saved New York; campaigns which dazzled German military critics and won the praise of Von Hindenburg.

Peremptorily demanding that the Washington government send him the regulars stationed near the Capital, O'Hagan with these and the "Hyphenated American Volunteers" of New York, slipped out of the city apparently in retreat to the South. Transferring his men by night in the Jersey meadows to the Erie Railroad–excepting the brigade which proceeded by automobile–he struck swiftly northward from Middletown, New York, through a valley which slopes toward the Hudson behind the almost impassable Shawangunk Mountains.

During the night of August 19th his forces reached the river at Kingston, surprising and overwhelming the enemy's ear guard. The invading forces were stretched in long lines down the Hudson, encamped in scattered battalions, while they moved their big guns into position near Mount Beacon to reduce West Point. It was the report of this unguarded alignment which had led O'Hagan to determine on this desperate stroke.

During the 20th and 21st, day and night, the Americans swept down both banks of the river, crossing on the Poughkeepsie Bridge, rounding up the enemy company by company, regiment by regiment, capturing their big guns and turning them, under the skilled hands of Americans trained in European armies, on those who had brought them. Down the river and across the rivers guns flashed and the battle raged. Late on the 21st the Americans crossed again to the west bank, and, joined by the West Point garrison, engaged the shaken but still superior forces of the enemy in the streets of Newburgh. The fury of freemen, aided by the enemy's own artillery, shelling them from across the river, was irresistible; General Sir Sam Hughes, the virulent Canadian enemy of the United States, beheld the remnants of his decimated 70,000 scattered and dispersed by 30,000 Americans.

A respite of three weeks had been given New York; by the second week of September 85,000 Canadians, Hindus, Japanese, French, and English were again coming down the Hudson, commanded by General Sir John French. O'Hagan awaited them, again with 30,000 men, near Kingston, at the mouth of the

Roundout Valley. As the invaders appeared the Americans withdrew up this valley. There was nothing for General French to do but detach 40,000 men to pursue them, while the rest of his force, with the big guns, advanced West Point. Retreating from one prepared position to another, O'Hagan led the enemy on, southward between the mountains, then westward over a broken plateau to a great, towering, terraced hill, which army engineers had meanwhile made a Gibraltar.

O'Hagan apparently permitted himself to be trapped there; but when the enemy came on with intent to storm this position, such showers of death met them that they recoiled, and sat down to a siege. But bigger guns than they had brought in pursuit had been embanked on that hill, so they had to retire to a safe distance and hope that starvation would reduce the Americans. But that had been prepared for by storing huge supplies of food on the hill, and by keeping one open narrow road to central New York. So Sir John French had to send some of his big guns from their positions before West Point. Laboriously they were brought and placed in position on October 3rd. Then O'Hagan, sacrificing his guns and some 6,000 of his men, successfully drew off his force through a mountain gorge so narrow that airmen could not detect it, into the frowning Catskills and over the divide into the valley of the Esopus, and so again to Kingston.

Then word was sent by wireless to the new force which New York City and its surrounding towns, during its second month of respite, had raised, drilled, and armed. Advancing from a base at Middletown, into the Roundabout Valley, it struck the enemy force retiring to Kingston after its hollow victory at East Hill, and this force, trapped between the new volunteers and O'Hagan's veterans, surrendered.

General French ordered 30,000 reinforcements, which were coming down the Hudson, to enter the Roundabout Valley and trap O'Hagan; but these, surprised by his appearance in double the expected force, quickly scattered. The Americans pursued them up the Hudson to Albany, capturing enroute great stores of munitions and supplies, totally cutting off General French's army before West Point. The latter began a distressed retreat, and caught between O'Hagan and the reinforced West Point garrison, surrendered on the 8th of November.

The crushing defeat of the invaders of New York really

paralyzed the Allies. England, realizing that she had again courted disaster by saving her own precious men while sending allies and colonials to fight her own battles, now sent expeditions to Canada. Canadian submarines, which, in violation of the treaty between England and the United States, had been in the Great Lakes since 1915, suddenly attacked shipping in the harbors of Chicago, Cleveland, and other lake cities, while expeditions landed in Detroit and Buffalo, ruthlessly suppressed citizen resistance, and built lines of trenches and redoubts around those cities. An English force penetrated from Eric, Pa., as far as Pittsburgh, but was halted before that important manufacturing city.

The Japanese and Mexicans, who had swept through Texas, joined with French Marines and Turkos and compelled the surrender of New Orleans and the army of General Barry. Jap and Mexicans withdrew westward, the others pushed up the Mississippi. The Turkos, aided by British West Indian negro agitators, stirred up terrible black revolts in the South, which were only suppressed by the loyalty of the masses of the negroes.

St. Louis was captured after a stubborn resistance, but at Cairo the invaders were halted by a volunteer army. A force of

Northwestern Mounted Police, which had struck down the Red River of the North and the Great Northern Railway, destroying millions of bushels of grain, was called back to suppress a revolt of American and German farmers in Western Canada. The situation of the Union was still precarious; it was split in several directions, its chief food-producing states cut off from the great consuming cities, its metal district and cotton belt cut off from the producing centers; but the enemies offensive power had gone.

America had rallied. Arms, munitions, supplies were being produced in almost sufficient quantities; armies had been drilled. From Kentucky and Tennessee came grim mountaineers; from the cities came the Germans, Scandinavians, and Irish; from mine and mill rallied Hungarian, Bohemian, Russian, Italian, Welshman, Scot, Pole, and Slovak; the Jews sent brigades which earned undying glory; from farm and ranch the scions of those Americans who had won the Revolution hastened to battle the one eternal enemy of American liberty. Trench to trench they faced the foe, at Lake Champlain, Buffalo, Cleveland, Pittsburgh, Cairo, and along the ridges of the Rockies.

The English, having been chiefly busy capturing

American markets, had neglected to provide adequately for their munitions supplies, and now purchased huge quantities in Germany. This was profitable business for Germany, and new plans sprang up. The trade became so notorious that the United States protested. The German government replied that German manufacturers had a legal right to supply munitions to all purchasers, and would gladly sell to America only that, unfortunately, England ruled the seas. The German government sustained its position with many apt quotations from the notes Mr. Wilson and Mr. Lansing had sent to Germany and Austria-Hungary in reply to their protests against the American trade in death during the Great War, and from the speeches of Mr. Roosevelt and the editorials of American newspapers. But while the American government was unable to answer, the heart of American burned with indignation as they saw German shells and bullets make American corpses, American invalids, and American widows and orphans.

In the midst of this situation, the great English liner *Mauretania*, especially constructed with English government money on lines that made her adaptable for transport purposes, officially a part of the English navy, was supposed to be armed, was sunk by an American submarine off Halifax. Among those lost were about one hundred German citizens, most of them contractors on their way to Canada to confer with military commanders about munition needs. The American government issued a statement showing the naval character of the *Mauretania,* and that she carried great quantities of munitions, reservists, and contractors, and was, therefore, a legitimate object of attack. The German government, however, issued a threatening note, practically demanding that the United States cease to use its new submarines, its only means of naval defense.

But there had been growing in Germany a strong sentiment against the export of munitions to the Allies. Led by Dr. Bernhard Dernberg, this movement at last won the support of the leading newspapers and public men. Dr. Dernberg pointed out that it was the German munitions on board the *Mauretania* which had been responsible for the submarine attack and for the explosion which sank the ship in ten minutes. The keen and fair-minded German people saw that the situation of 1915, when Germany and America came near to war over the *Lusitania* and *Arabic* incidents and export of American munitions to the Allies, was now reversed. The second German note to the American government admitted the necessity and rights of the American submarine warfare, and promised effective steps to prevent German citizens sailing on ships containing munitions of war. And on January 1, 1921, the German people celebrated a new humanitarian era, as the law passed by the Bundesrath forbidding the sale of implements of warfare to any nation at war, became effective.

My readers will remember that the English press, and the Continental press through English sources, reeked with stories of American atrocities from the day that England declared war. But when the Allied invasion began to fail, the turgid stream of abuse swelled to an angry torrent; and the climax was reached when the Americans began to use the "flying dragon."

The "flying dragon" was invented by that great American genius, Hudson Maxim. It is an aerial torpedo sustained by wings, propelled by a motor, and charged with an incomparably deadly gas, guided by wireless waves, and exploded either by contact or by wireless detonation. I have seen this deadly engine in operation, guided surely to its place by a wireless operator toying with little electrical keys in an observatory, bringing death to whole battalions, turning trenches into graves of hundreds of men distorted into every posture of agony. Every factory was put to work turning out these engines, and soon the trenches of the invaders were being steadily pushed back at every point. And the English, ignoring their own use of gas bombs, shrieked that Americans were "a race of barbarians who have forfeited their place among civilized nations."

I had the sad pleasure of putting before German readers the facts of Allied atrocities in this war; the burning of homes and cities, the cruel fate of thousands of women and girls, the savage repression of the patriots of California, the hideous negro uprising, and all the nameless cruelties inflicted on a white people by other whites and their Japanese, Mexican, Hindu, and Senegalese mercenaries, to further the plots of the gang of English politicians for whom humanity blushes!

The next installment will show how the United States and Germany freed the world.

America and Germany Restore Freedom to Land and Sea

XII

I need not rehearse in detail the developments which led to the intervention of Germany in behalf of the United States; but I am able to throw a certain light on occurrences in America during the weeks immediately preceding our entrance into the conflict.

The masses of American people had responded to the call made upon their patriotism and courage with a sort of holy zeal. Out of the heroic past, out of all the traditions of America, that spirit which England for twenty-five years had sought to crush under the weight of corrupted journals, falsified histories, and snobbish public utterances, arose and resumed the only real struggle America had ever made, against the only foe America ever had, England—England the tyrant of 1776, the pirate of 1812, the assassin of 1863, the false friend of 1898 and 1915, and the murderer of 1920.

But no sooner had the first onset of the engirdling hosts been haled than the Tory raised his head, and by all the secret and subtle means at his disposal, intrigued to bring about a peace which would permit England to withdraw unpunished, to carry away billions of loot from the scenes of her devastating passage, retain her West Indies, and enter into an alliance with the United States against Japan, on terms which were to include the neutralization of the Panama Canal and the recognition of England's equal rights with the United States in Mexico.

The disclosure of this Tory plot was forced prematurely by the appointment of a commission which Congress, in secret session, had authorized to go to Germany with certain information and propositions.

During his last week of service in the House, after his victorious campaign and before he resigned to accept the rank of Major-General in the Regular Army, Shawn O'Hagan had secured the appointment of this commission. It consisted of B. Herman Ridder, who had succeeded his father as editor of the New York *Staats-Zeitung;* Horace L. Brand of the Illinois *Staats-Zeitung,* Professor Hugo Muensterberg; Dr. C. J. Hexamer, President of the German-American Alliance; the ever youthful poet Sylvester Viereck, who had worked so intelligently for the cause of the Fatherland; William Bayard Hale, the great publisher; and James K. McGuire, the wealthy contractor and ex-Mayor of Syracuse, N.Y., whose book, The King, the Kaiser and Irish Freedom, had done so much to consolidate German-Irish understanding.

The workings of the new Tory plot were quickly detected by the keener patriotic leaders, and when, in a panic over the appointment of the Commission to Germany, the traitors began to fill the newspapers with articles favoring such peace with England as I have outlined, it was evident, since the press was under the control of a National Censor, that the plot was reaching high personages and powers in Washington.

Then the true voice of American patriotism spoke a decisive word, again through the man of determination and force, General O'Hagan. As Commander of the Army of the East he sent to Congress, and circulated throughout the country, the following open letter:

"It has come to be a matter of common knowledge that certain interests are working, in Congress and through every agency by which they may hope to sway the Government and betray the people, to bring about a peace with England on terms which include the retention by England of all her loot; the retention by England of all her American dominions, including her newly stolen half of Mexico; and the neutralization of the Panama Canal. It is understood that the bribe offered the American people to induce them to agree to this infamous proposal is English help against the Yellow conquerors of California.

"On behalf of the officers and men of the Army of the East, and expressing also what we have learned to be the sentiments of the Army of the West, I denounce this proposition as treason, and I denounce those who make it as traitors.

"The history of the United States from the troublous days of its revolutionary conception and birth till to-day is the history of English plans of exploitation. England brought on this war. But I will not insult the American people by assuming to convince them of truths which burn in every heart like white-hot coals.

"Rather I hereby announce on behalf of the Army of the East that the only terms upon which peace will be made with England are these: The expulsion of England from all possessions on either American continent and from all islands in the Western Hemisphere; the attainment of guarantees, with such conditions as will prevent evasion by England, of the Freedom of the Seas; and the collection from England of an indemnity which will pay, as far as money can pay, for the robberies and atrocities committed by the English and Canadians in our country.

"It is not meet that an army should assume any attitude toward its government but implicit obedience. To-day, however, the American armies are the American people, and in the midst of this dreadful crisis, with our lives and the life of the Republic at stake, it is our duty to speak and act decisively for the preservation of our liberty and honor.

"It is the decision of the Army of the East that the war against

England must be prosecuted to the result I have indicated, and the army will not omit any word or deed necessary to secure this result and protect the Republic against enemies, foreign or domestic, according to our sacred oath."

The vast majority of Congress were, of course, of the same mind as the army and the people, and this virile proclamation, unmasking the plotters, put patriots on their guard; and the last English intrigue against the American Republic died in its birth-throes.

Outside America, the first result of this public discourse of the English plans was the blowing up of the Suez Canal by Japanese cruisers, and the withdrawal of Japanese troops from the Allied lines in the East; they marched across Canada to their "Pacific Provinces," and the English, Canadians, and French dared not oppose them as, with weakened forces, they strove to hold back the advancing American lines.

England and Japan, thus suddenly transferred into enemies, were both feverishly seeking the alliance of Germany; but the German Government was equally deaf to the rival assassins. England, indeed, had just before this issued an Order in Council absolutely prohibiting neutral vessels from entering or leaving American ports with any sort of cargo whatsoever. It will be remembered that several German ships were seized. Germany at once protested in no uncertain tones, whereupon England sought to make a deal, offering Germany extraordinary trade privileges throughout the British Empire, a free hand in Russia and the Balkans, and secretly, a promise of French colonies after French usefulness to England was over; all this in return for German assistance against America.

But the American Commission had now arrived in Germany, the American position was firmly revealed to the German Government and people, and the proofs of the orgy of Allied atrocities were put before them. Germany's answer was given on February 12th, the birthday of Abraham Lincoln, the great American President of German descent.

Speaking to the Bundesrath and the Reichstag, Chancellor von Bethmann-Hollweg said the time had come to do two things: to end the Yellow Peril which had at last fulfilled the fears of the White Race by overrunning a White Man's country; and to end the Red Peril of the English Empire which, during four centuries, had carried oppression and tyranny to every quarter of the world, crushing nationality, destroying industry, debauching politics, elevating hypocrisy, putting out the lights of education and culture, promoting famine, crushing resistance with bloody hands, and tying vast populations to the politic-economic machine of the Empire, for the benefit of English capitalists alone.

What followed is history.

The German fleets were already at sea, and on receipt of wireless orders they fell like avenging furies on Jellicoe's division of the English Navy in North America; sending some to the bottom, the rest scuttling southward. Admiral Beatty's powerful fleet blockading the Virginia Capes and the Carolina and Georgia coasts joined Jellico's remnants, but still the pursuing Teuton avengers were in superior force, and the English fled to the Caribbean. There they were joined by their equally powerful fleet which had been blockading the Canal.

But by vast labors the Americans in the Canal Zone, while holding back a Colombian army and bands of Panama bandits, had cleared away the man-made mountain which had filled the Culebra Cut. Now the American fleet sailed eagerly out, with their German allies. There followed the greatest naval battle in history, in which practically the entire English navy, which had so long held a trembling world in awe, was shattered and sunk, to the rejoicing of men and angels!

The German and American fleets turned east and north, and on March 17th–St. Patrick's Day–off the coast of Ireland, the last remnants of England's maritime power were sunk, and ere the smoke of battle cleared away, the commanders of the American and German fleets, by order of their governments, proclaimed Ireland a free and independent nation.

After that the occupation of England, the swift capture of Paris, the bringing of Russia to her knees, the liberation of India and South Africa.

The German-American fleets again crossed the Atlantic, destroyed enroute the French warships that had been ruling the Gulf of Mexico, passed through the Panama Canal, and pursued the Japanese navy across the Pacific, diving it and destroying one part of it near Hawaii, the other off Manila. The bulk of the German-American fleet remained blockading the Island Empire.

The French forces near Cairo soon surrendered after their

squadron withdrew from the Gulf. Along the northern border the Canadian-English-French forces were steadily being rolled back before the Flying Dragons and the bayonet charges of the Americans; and at last England and France had to make terms, as we have seen. Canada was instituted as a Republic, bound by treat to alliance with the United States, forbidden to ally herself with England in any way or degree. The British West Indies became the property of the United States.

The Japanese forces were now cut off from their empire, while a million Americans assaulted their tremendously fortified positions commanding every pass through the Rockies, launching Flying Dragons against them, bringing ever more heavy artillery to bear; till they were dislodged and divided, those who were in the northern ranges being captured, those in the south driven to Mexico. A few months of determined warfare subjugated Mexico, which was taken under the protection of the United States to be reorganized in anticipation of setting it free at the earliest possible moment; reforms being granted to the peons, and American and Germany capital invited in under government regulation.

On July 4, 1921, a treaty of peace was signed between Japan, the United States, and Germany. The Japanese gave up all claims to special privileges alike in China and Mexico, bound themselves to restrict their navy, and, very sensibly, were permitted to purchase the Philippines for a good round sum, guaranteeing to continue for the benefit of the Filipinos the beneficent measures inaugurated by the Americans.

The Russians and Canadians evacuated Alaska, and the portions of that territory, which some years before had been added to Canada by Anglo-maniac American statesmen, were restored to their proper sovereignty.

Australia and New Zealand had, after the break between England and Japan, suffered for a short time the terrors of Yellow Domination which had delighted them as applied to America; but when the Japs sailed into their bays and took possession of their cities, they were a wiser and sadder people. American and Germany wisely insisted that Japan evacuate the former British colonies, which were erected into Republics.

To-day the world is a fairer and more hopeful place than ever before in history. The Yellow Race is no longer in any part subject to the oppression of the White, nor is it imbued with any desire to triumph over the White.

The world is under the hegemony of the United States and Germany, the two nations cherishing the highest ideals and capable of the greatest achievements.

The monstrous Red Empire is no more; it is only a bad memory to the world. The people of England, at last rid of the delusions by which their own exploiters induced them to exploit the world, are learning, we may hope, to achieve civilization, happiness and content as one of the family of nations.

And Ireland, India, South Africa, Canada, Australia, and New Zealand are flourishing and expanding in the air of freedom.

America and Germany have liberated the world!

The end.

The Story of the War of 1920

By the Author of "A Trip to Headline Land"

Must the United States Fight Another Big War?

Will It Come Within Five Years?

Will the Enemy Be The Allies—England, Japan, France, Russia?

Will They Overrun America with Japs, Hindus, Cossacks and Senegalese?

Will They Murder, Ravish, Burn and Loot?

Y E S !

What Are The Conditions That Make This Inevitable?

How Will English and Japanese Diplomacy Bring It About?

How Will the English Press Justify It to the World?

What Will Be the Result?

Read about it in
The
Fatherland

Beginning shortly
in The Fatherland

We are being girt by a Ring of Iron!   Some day it will close about us!   We shall be battling for our very lives!   And the English will call us "Barbarians" and accuse us of violating the "neutrality" of "small nations" and committing "atrocities."

Read This Prophetic Story

Subscribe to The Fatherland now so that you will not miss this big feature.

Teaser for "The War of 1920" in the Fatherland Vol 2 Issue 20.

Made in the USA
Las Vegas, NV
08 June 2023